Liberty

Fighting Crime in America's Off-World State

Credits

2300AD Original Writers and Contributors
Marc Miller, Loren Wiseman, Frank Chadwick, Lester Smith, Timothy Brown, Gary Thomas, Joe Fugate, John Harshman, William H. Keith, Jr. Deb Zeigler, Bryan Gibson and Steve Venters

Author
Wesley Street

Line Manager
Colin Dunn

Editor
Matthew Sprange

Layout
Amy Perrett

Cover Illustration
Amy Perrett

Interior Illustrations
Amy Perrett

The American Exploration and Colonisation Authority (AECA) created by Clay Johanson, and used with permission

Contents

Introduction

The colony of Ellis is the pride of the United States. America's newest state has grown into the largest and most important colony in the American Arm. Hard work, ingenuity and persistence turned a desert planet into a breadbasket.

While the future seems nothing but bright for Ellis, the colony has serious problems. Crime is on the rise as the planet's population grows. Smuggling is as endemic on Ellis as any world in the American Arm. The supremacist New America movement, thought dead since the post-Twilight Era recovery, has found fertile soil in which to spread its message of isolationism and intolerance.

Liberty: Fighting Crime in America's Off-World State is a sourcebook and two adventures for *2300AD*. It outlines the culture and politics of Ellis's state capital, Liberty, and several of its prominent citizens. The first adventure, Profit Without Honour, places the player characters in the roles of federal agents investigating a major drug trafficking ring. In the second adventure, Desert and Reward, the player characters hunt for a hidden compound full of New America fanatics.

This books references pieces of equipment from *Tools for Frontier Living* and *Hard Suits, Combat Walkers and Battlesuits*.

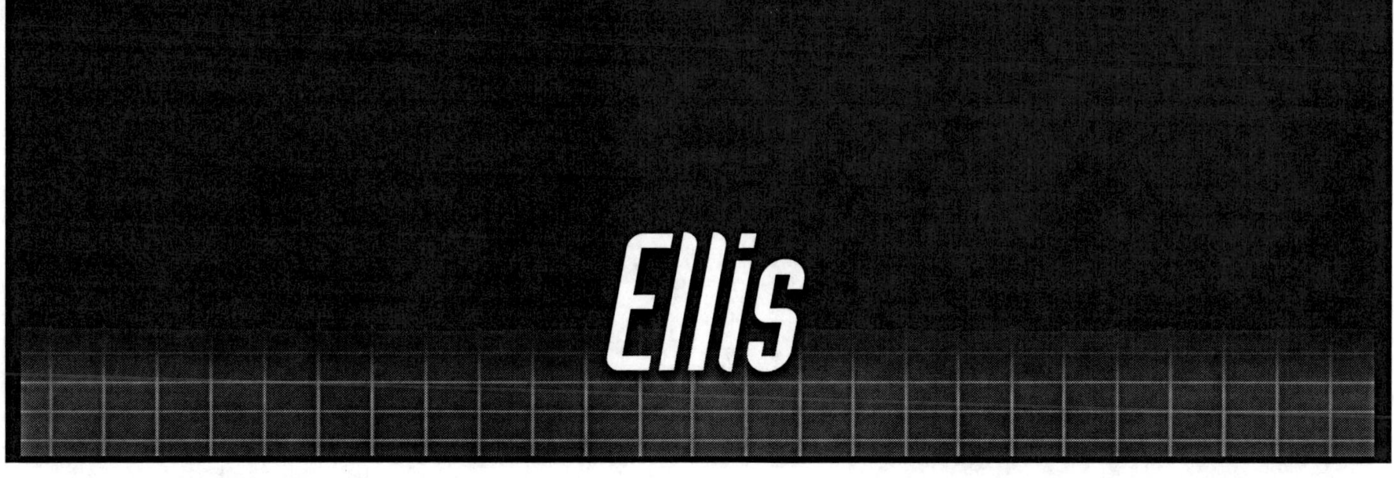

Ellis

I remember Dad was excited that we were granted an emigration permit. When the boredom of his part time data management job weighed him down, he sang the AECA ad jingle:

Off we goooooooo!
A new land of ad-ven-true!
Off we goooooooo!
Opportunity a-waaaaaaits!

We moved off Earth to Ellis when I was seven. I don't remember much about the trip out other than when I woke up crying I couldn't make tears. And I rarely had to use the toilet.

We worked on Uncle Harmon's ranch, just outside the capital. We tended jackrabbits for meat and fur. It wasn't as much fun as you might think. The gene-mods that made the hares hardy enough to survive in a desert also made them extremely aggressive. A little kid was an easy target for claws and blunt teeth.

Mom and Dad disappeared when I was twelve. No explanation. Harmon kept me around and taught me how to shoot a rifle. When he couldn't keep his perverted hands to himself, I left.

A 14 year-old on the streets of Cincinnati was a potential victim. But Ellis didn't deal with the kind of crimes the Core was known for. A lot of people moved to the colony so that the government and the corporations weren't always looking over their shoulders. That meant almost anything was permitted, so long as it didn't hurt someone else. No force in the universe could send me back to a farm but a kid without technical skills wasn't much use otherwise. I needed money if I wanted to keep my freedom.

I impressed Thom when I beat up a member of his crew. The kid was blitzed on some tweaked hash and wanted to make time with me. Thom was more impressed with how I handled a gun. He took me on as an employee and I've been dealing Scribble since. The money is fantastic, the sheriff's deputies are a joke and the glassy-eyed farmers, townsfolk and ranchers respect you. Or fear you which, honestly, is kind of awesome. My only worry is keeping the money flowing but the product I sell practically moves itself. Beats skinning jackrabbits.

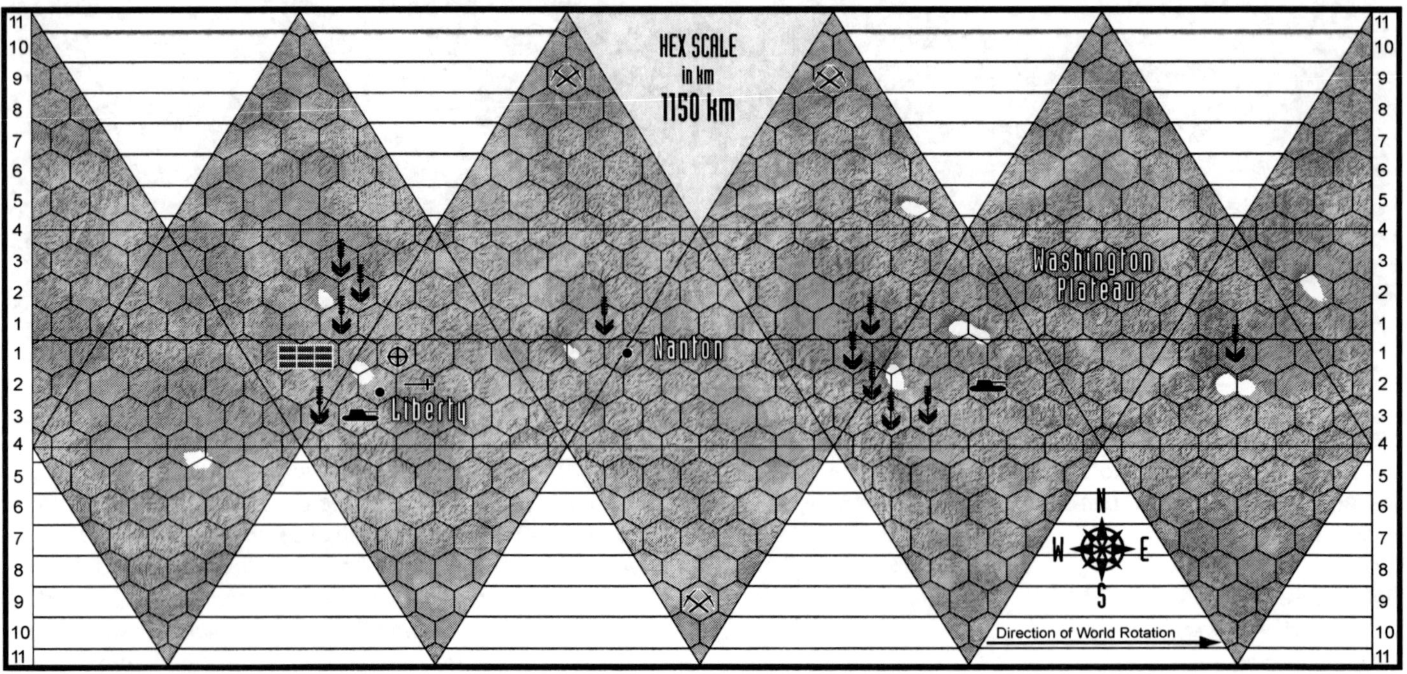

Legend

- Major City
- Spaceport
- Catapult
- Mining
- Farming
- Military Base
- Fusion Plant
- Solar Power Rectenna
- Heavy Industry

Ellis is the first of three worlds orbiting a M3 VI red dwarf star. Located 23.6 light years from Sol, Ellis is the terminating human settlement in the American Sub-Arm. The system primary is very cool resulting in a tight ecosphere. Ellis's orbital distance of 0.07 AU hid the planet from detection until an American survey mission entered the system in 2220. Later that year, the exploration vessel *Kathryn Lynn* conducted the first manned landings and research expeditions on the planet's surface.

The system is rounded out by two gas giants, Oyster, which sits at 0.15 AU, and Gibbet at 0.27 AU. Both planets sport multiple natural satellites. Oyster's largest moon, the Titan-like Carlton, hosts a United States Marine Corps low-gravity and non-terrestrial combat centre. Gibbet's largest satellite is home to a joint American-Australian research base dedicated to studying the Jovian planet.

Ellis's close proximity to its primary combined with its strong magnetosphere prevents standard shuttles and other vessels from safely orbiting or landing. To compensate, Ellis's primary spaceport facility is located on Boise, a spun asteroid located in Oyster's trailing trojans. Shuttles specially hardened against radiation run cargo and passengers to and from Ellis and Boise.

SYSTEM DATA

Primary Name: AC +48 1595 89
Spectral Class: M3 VI
Stellar Mass: 0.013
Magnitude: 10.97
X, Y, Z Coordinates: -6.5, -14.3, 17.6
Number of Planets: 3
Number of Asteroid Belts: 0

Primary Stutterwarp Threshold: 0.279 AU

Ellis is classified as a post-garden world. Once Earth-like, the planet's ecology has degraded over the eons with microscopic animals, lichens and mosses remaining as the sole indigenous species. Though there are thought to be hidden aquifers and deep rift valley rivers, only 7% of the planet's surface area holds standing water. This is limited to a series of small, briny and highly-salinised lakes in the southern hemisphere.

Ellis is a desert. Its minimal axial tilt results in a stable climate and the planet has very limited tectonic motion, primarily in the form of moderately active shield volcanoes. However Ellis is a very old planet and what few mountain ranges remain have been ground down by weathering. The terrain is a mixture of dusty wastelands and fields of boulders and gravel. Dry riverbeds are scattered across the planet which indicate that Ellis was once blessed with a great deal of flowing water. Extreme desert survival wear or DNA modification is a requirement for colonists as the planet's climate is dangerous for the unprotected.

As there is not enough plant life to replenish oxygen, Ellis has been losing it over time to the oxidation of minerals. Scientists believe that Ellis may have been victim of a major extinction-level event that killed much of the plant life millennia ago. As Ellis's sun is one of the most stable stars in known space it is unlikely the event was caused by extreme solar activity.

As the 50th state of the union, Ellis is America's pride and joy and the bread basket of the American Arm. Despite the success of the colony project, the planet is still largely unexplored. More complex forms of life and answers to other scientific mysteries may be present somewhere on Ellis.

Planetary Data

UWP: B861666-9 De
Name: Ellis
Distance from Primary: 0.07 AU (Tidally-locked)
Year Length: 2.44 days
Sise: 12,850 km in diameter
Day Length: 18.02 hours
World Type: Rocky
Surface Gravity: 0.99 G
Atmospheric Pressure: 1.4 ATM
Climate: Temperate
Water Presence: 7%
Atmospheric Composition: N_2 (80%), O_2 (16%), Trace Gases (4%)
Satellites: 0
Biosphere: 1
Compatibility: 8
Natural Resources: 4 (Light Metals and Agricultural Products)
Habitability: 6
Tectonics: 4
Tides: N/A

Colony Data

UCP: B975644-A Ri De 5 0
Colony Type: Agricultural
Interface Capability: Catapult, Spaceplane
Colony Area: 2.2 million km^2
Transportation Network: 7 (60% of colony connected by excellent road network)
Telecommunications Network: 5 (Low-speed data connectivity to all of colony, high-speed (Link) connectivity to 10% of colony)
Colony Population: 4.5 million
Government Type: Representative Democracy
Law Level: Moderate (Assault Weapons Prohibited)
Tech Level: 10 (current production capability)
Agriculture: 8
Mining: 6
Industry: 4
Date Founded: 2228
Nationality: American
Life Expectancy: 95 years
Major Cities: Liberty (125,000)
Trade Data: Rich
Principal Trading Partners: American colonies, Australian colonies, America, Australia
Resources: Agriculture, Petrochemicals
Bases: Military Base, Naval Base, Foundation Facility (Alberta Farmer's Cooperative)
Services: Fusion Plant, Road Net (60%), Rail Net (60%), Link Network (10%), Weather Satellites, Communications Satellites, Orbital Terminal (Boise)

Liberty

Liberty Spaceport
Chatham Arch
Eagle's Nest
Mars Hill
Haughville
Lilly
Babe
Herron
Saint Claire
Morton
Freedom
Fall Creek
Meridian
Brookside
Holy Rosary
LAKE FELLOWSHIP
Hawthorne
Springdale
Stringtown
Cottage Home
Arsenal
Lockerbie
Irish Hill
Tear
Columbia
Cole
Bunch
Independence
Irvington
Pike
Geist
Maywood
Dale
Jolietville
Lebanon
Upper Canal
Concord
Nora
Fletcher
Troy
Noblesville
Mapleton
Benjamin
Spiceland
Westfield
Mt. Carmel
Julietta
Cicero
Liberty
Crawfordsville
Holy Cross
Eagletown
Monticello
Fort Patton
Perry
Speedway
St. Vincent
Westwood
Ben Davis
LIBERTY COUNTY AREA
Key
Canal
Capitol City
City
Town/Village
State Highway
County Highway
Main Rail Line
Secondary Rail Line
Hex scale in km
30 km
BEECH GROVE CANYON

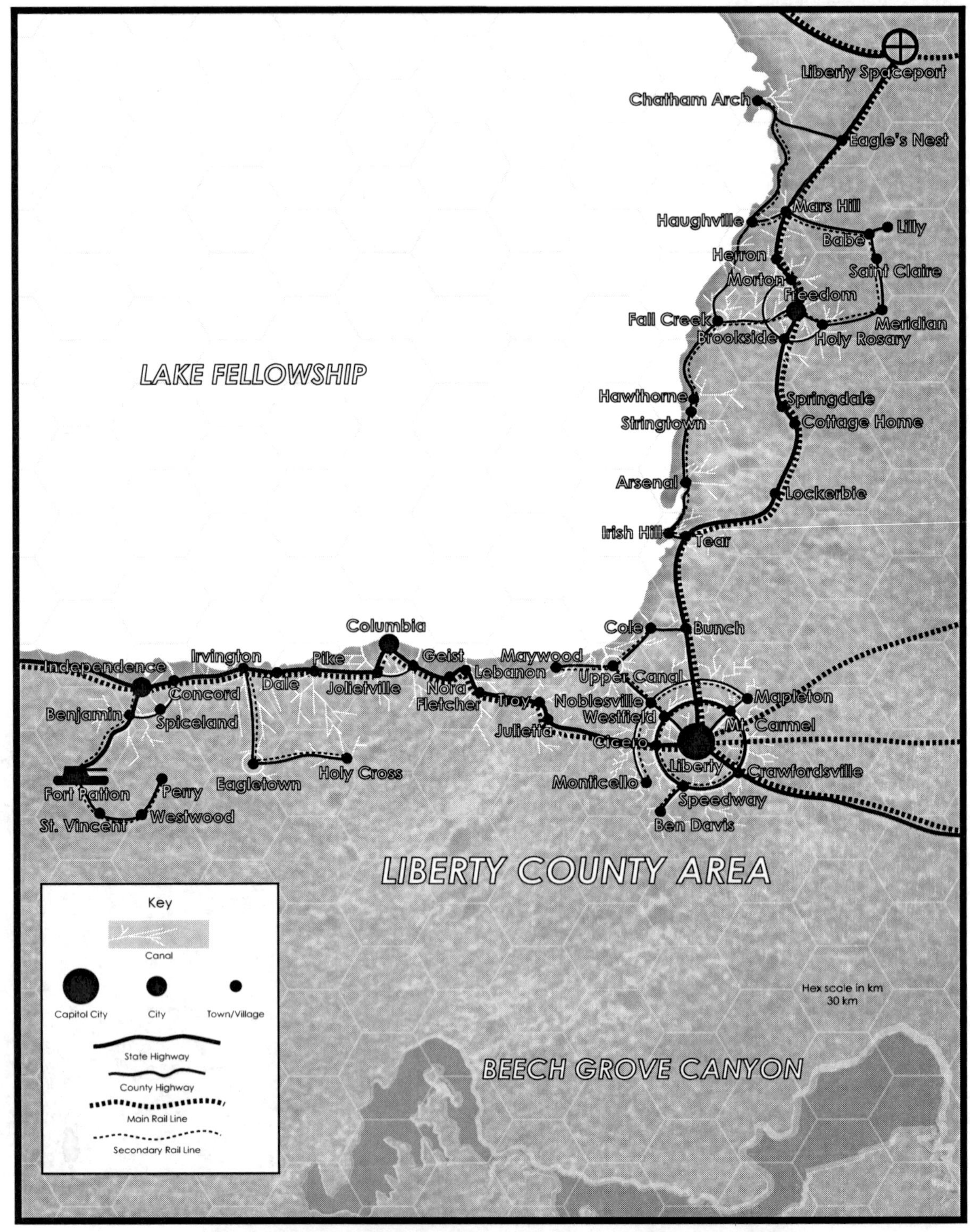

Settlement

After the *Kathryn Lynn* returned to Earth in February 2221, Captain William 'Buck' Mossburg filed a conclusive survey report with the US Department of Extraplanetary Resources (USDER). Included was a recommendation for the establishment of a scientific outpost on Ellis to study the planet's failing ecology. The American government was hesitant to sink time and resources into a world that was well-past its prime life-supporting days. When the survey was made public, the North American Research League immediately applied pressure to not only establish a fully-functioning colony, but to investigate methods to revive Ellis's ecology. NARL concluded that the end of all life on Ellis was near and that the American government had a moral imperative to make the planet habitable once more. The American Extrasolar Colonial Administration (AECA) consulted with NARL and other scientific foundations and put together a list of recommendations for a full-scale planetary engineering project. The American government contracted the Alberta Farmers' Collective to spearhead the efforts on Ellis.

In 2228, a pathfinder team, headed by Logan Bearspow and Avery Walker-Olson, arrived in Ellis orbit aboard the Canadian colony transport *Digby*. The site for Liberty, the first permanent base, was selected due to its immediate proximity to water and nearness to the equator. The second wave of pathfinder colonists were scheduled to arrive in just over one year resulting in the initial team facing an aggressive deadline.

After a temporary camp shelter was constructed, surveyors and engineers, working from plans drawn by satellites, orbital flyovers and the *Kathryn Lynn* expedition, began work on Liberty's primary habitat domes. Ellis's mix of atmospheric gases and air pressure was within unmodified human comfort levels but Liberty's equatorial position and the planet's sparse hydrosphere led to exceptional radiation loss. Daytime temperatures reached as high as 36°C and fell to 5°C at night. Ellis's lack of water and flat terrain also resulted in high wind-generated dust storms.

For safety and comfort, Liberty was designed as a sub-surface settlement. Minimal tectonic activity allowed engineers to carve out a series of naturally cooled atria, galleries, souks, warrens and transit corridors without fear of collapse. Wide domes were erected to provide natural light to spacious atriums below with mirrors reflecting it throughout the settlement. Electrostatic repulsion systems prevented the planet's talcum powder-like fines from adhering to the domes' surfaces. Liberty expanded this network of warrens and domes with subsequent influxes of colonists. By the 2270s, immigration reached equilibrium with available temporary housing space and Liberty's physical spread slowed.

As construction of the colony centre began, other teams staked out the initial farm plots that would be necessary to keep the colony fed. A system of artificial windbreaks was built to protect Liberty and the farm communities that surrounded it. The earliest farms were built near Lake Fellowship and the series of solar- or fusion-powered desalinisation plants that converted the briny, salt-covered lake water into a product potable to both humans and plants. As the colony grew, more aqueducts were cut to service newer farms.

When the first wave of American settlers landed in 2229 they found a fully-functional community ready for occupants. After they filtered through the AECA Homestead office in Liberty they took control of their land shares, converted the regolith to functioning soil and produced crops. As of 2300, Liberty has surpassed a population count of 125,000 but is only slightly larger than Ellis's 40-plus other cities. It serves as both the colony's state capitol and as the irrigation network central hub for several county-wide 'daughter' communities; smaller cities and towns hugging Lake Fellowship.

Locations and Culture

As state capitol and the largest city on Ellis, Liberty is the colony's centre for governance, business and entertainment. Culture and food critics would find the city lacking compared to the megacities of the Core but it serves the needs of a colonial population at the far end of American space. Free standing architecture is primarily influenced by Pueblo Revival- and American Prairie-styles. Corners are rounded and hand-made ceramic ornamentation is common. Buildings outside the domes tend to be very horizontal with flat roofs. Government buildings follow the traditional American neoclassical style.

The city's population is divided into three segments – government employees, industrial/service workers and transients. The transient population consists of immigrants waiting on the USDER to assign land plots and resources to these new farmers.

United States government offices and the local US District Courthouse fill the Sen. Evan Whitcomb Federal Complex. Tenants include the AECA, Centres for Disease Control and Prevention (CDCP), Treasury Extra-National Crimes Bureau (TEN-B), Interstellar Commerce Monitoring Network (ICMN), Veterans Benefits Administration (VBA) and the National Security Office (NSO). The American Intelligence Service (AIS) occupies a secured administrative office in the sprawling building but prefers to avoid advertising this to the public.

The Federal Complex is guarded by the US Marshal Service (USMS). It is monitored by security robots and armed deputies are on duty at all time. For those without access to Link technology, automated kiosks outside the building handle inquiries and claims processing and remote clerks are always available. Defendants accused of breaking federal statutes are held in a secured wing of the complex before and during trial. As Ellis is a formal state, it does not technically deport colonists but rather transfers them to the care of a Bureau of Criminal Rehabilitation (BCR) facility on Earth for processing. The closed and detached nature of the Federal Complex serves to stir suspicion among the residents of Ellis and helps fuel paranoia regarding government overreach and secrecy.

The Ellis Statehouse, the state capitol building of Ellis, is located in the centre of Liberty proper. The building was the original home of the colonial administration government. It was rebuilt in a more traditional American style in 2275 after the referendum for Ellis's statehood was passed. Materials used were indigenous to the planet including various stones and copper. Ellis has a bicameral legislative body and the Statehouse is built to accommodate the two houses – a wing is set aside for the upper house state senate and another for the lower house state representatives. Both wings are joined in the middle by a large atrium and rotunda which is used for receptions and the offices of the Ellis Supreme Court and the Court of Appeal. The multi-story atrium is decorated with bronze and stone busts and plaques commemorating Ellis politicians and leaders. Large murals celebrate exploration and settlement of the planet. A scale model of the *Kathryn Lynn* sits on the atrium floor beneath a holographic projection of William Mossburg.

The Ellis State Office is cattycorner to the Statehouse and houses all of the local bureaucratic offices including the governor's office, various licensing agencies and the Ellis State Police headquarters. The governor's twenty-three room residence is located across an expanse of manicured parkland from the Statehouse. Protection of the governor and the residence along with state-occupied buildings is the purview of the Ellis State Police (ESP). Uniformed state police troopers are distinctive with their high crowned campaign hats, leather cords and knee-high polished boots.

Liberty City Hall is a wedge-shaped warren located in the main tunnel linking Liberty's two oldest domes. Offices and conference rooms for Mayor Spencer Hart's administration, along with the city-county council, occupy the facility's top level. The ground level is primarily judicial chambers for the local court system including elected judges, the coroner, the prosecutor's office and the public defender's office. The central two levels are for the use of various city bureaucracies such as assessors, clerks, recorders, surveyors and media relations.

Liberty County Sheriff's Department headquarters is attached to City Hall and includes jail facilities for those accused and awaiting local trial. Convicted criminals are transferred to the Department of Corrections at the Ellis State Penitentiary in Independence. LCSD jurisdiction extends over the entirety of Liberty County, so a network of stations provides bases of operation for local sheriff units. Uniformed officers wear a combination of slate grey trousers and jacket with black trim, matching the local terrain, along with a black ball cap. Detectives and other plain clothes units wear the traditional business dress attire of law enforcement officers throughout human space. Sheriff investigations reflect the Liberty area's rural nature. The most common crimes are theft, domestic abuse, public intoxication and assault and battery.

Criminals from marginalised populations in the Core are traditionally spawned from greed and economic desperation. While greed is certainly a motivating factor in Liberty's criminal DNA, crime is predominantly a cultural artefact. Ellis colonists share sharply different political and social philosophies from Core Americans. On Ellis, a political class is considered a necessary evil and at worst it is an anachronistic chokehold, rife with abuse and corruption. Economic opportunity is plentiful so many in Liberty's criminal set justify their sociopathic behaviours as rebellion against a distant, meddling and uncaring state.

Few criminals operate independently. Most band together into small, eight-to-ten person crews. Many crews are specialists and are temporarily hired by larger organised crime syndicates, such as the American Mafia or the Freihafen Black Hand. Liberty-area organised criminal activity is usually associated with smuggling, possession and distribution of controlled substances and contraband.

Liberty Union Station, the primary passenger rail depot, is located on the southern edge of Liberty. Operated by the AmLev Rail & Depot Company, several transportation concerns have been assigned trackage rights to the station. Union Station is a heavily trafficked location as the maglev system serves as a physical connection between all the cities of the colony. Grains, vegetables and meat products from outlying farms and unprocessed ores arrive by rail and are sent to Liberty's many processing plants. Those products destined for off-world markets are loaded back on to trains and taken north to the mass driver catapult and Liberty Spaceport. Union Station's passenger terminal is clean and bright with a variety of lounge, restaurant, entertainment and shopping venues along with a large, mid-tier hotel. The Ellis State Police Transportation Authority Service monitors the movements of all terminal visitors. Union Station, along with various government office complexes in Liberty, is among the places where personal weapons are strictly prohibited.

Public transportation in Liberty consists of electric taxis, light automated people movers, rental bicycles and single-rider electric vehicles. Liberty does not utilise a TrafCon system, therefore taxis are driven by licensed, freelance operators. The LCSD conducts regular drone and vehicle patrols of all roadways to ensure safety.

The main campus of Ellis University is located in Liberty. The top institute of higher learning on the planet, the four-year university is heavily partnered with the Alberta Farmers' Collective. The most popular area of study is a cross-discipline program incorporating agricultural sciences and business. Physical sciences, including geology and planetology, and engineering are also common degrees. University policy requires that all students live on campus in order to foster community and immersive learning. EU is a major sponsor of a local community college program that supports technical and two-year study programs, such as hands-on maintenance and repair training as well as civil service instruction.

Though Ellis is light-years from the mother nation it embraces several of the historic past times of America. Sports and sporting events are a strong and unifying influence for most colonists. The reality and costs of long-distance stutterwarp travel makes interplanetary competition impractical, outside of exhibition games. Ellis sports rivalries are based around local leagues. The 15,000 seat AmeriCo Arena is the home to Liberty's local semi-professional athletic teams – the Liberty Chasers (basketball), the Liberty Miners (baseball), the Liberty Gunsmiths (American football) and the Liberty Geckos (soccer). AmeriCo Arena is also home to the Ellis University Fighting Governors sports program.

Ellis falls behind other states when it comes to the appreciation of contemporary culture but Liberty residents enjoy electronic gaming and entertainment as much as any other American. The colony has a near zero-percent unemployment rating and an extremely small leisure class. Because colonists are very occupied by day-to-day work, prevalent e-games tend to be previous-generation single-player titles or serialised interactive stories that do not require dedicated player bases. Augmented Reality games are a foreign concept in Liberty but Virtual Reality worlds are popular, especially re-creations of historical, tourist and nature sites on Earth. Because tangible wildlife is unknown on Ellis, VR fauna simulations from Earth and other American Arm settlements are as popular with Ellis children as dinosaur sims are to Earth children.

The Liberty Museum of Art primarily features works by Ellis-based artists though the occasional exhibit touring the American Arm will make its way through Liberty. The majority of pieces fall into the category of decorative arts, simple forms with a folk aesthetic. Sand castings and glass blowing are both popular approaches as an abundance of material and energy allows for easy moulding. Painting or laser etching on metal, such as industrial saw blades, is another common medium. The museum is home to a small theatre used for live performances by local musicians and actors.

Liberty offers a number of dining venues, including a small number of upscale eateries. The most popular restaurant offering is the bar-and-grill format. Rat meat and insect protein consumption along with vat-grown carniculture are common practices but in an agrarian community, meals featuring DNA modified cattle, goats, rabbits and fowl, are inexpensive and prevalent options. With water at a premium, brewing or distilling large batches of grain-based alcohol is prohibitively expensive. Dates, watermelon and wine grapes grow well in Ellis's arid climate making wine the drink of choice. Liberty's vintners are unable to penetrate the Core market but their stock is popular on outposts and colonies in the American Arm.

Spirituality and religion are important cultural touchstones for the citizens of Liberty. The city offers over 30 different venues for worship. These are primarily Protestant and unaffiliated Christian denominations, but the Liberty dioceses is the largest Catholic congregation on Ellis. Jewish, Islamic and Hindu worship venues are also available and welcomed. A typical resident judges others by words, deeds and strengths of character but even the most culturally progressive native will admit to an anti-atheist/anti-agnostic bias. Most natives believe that humbleness before a Creator, even a non-Christian one, is a sign of righteousness. Materialist Core attitudes are frowned upon.

Located on the western-most edge of Liberty County, near the city of Independence, is Fort Patton. It is the home of IV Corps Headquarters and its 11th Armoured Cavalry Regiment and 184th Infantry Brigade. The fort is also the operational headquarters for American Arm Command (AMARMCOM). Fort Patton is an undesirable posting for troops from the Core worlds. Ellis's barren and lifeless terrain is considered very unpleasant and the assignment requires all posted to undergo DNA modification for maximum combat readiness. The US government compensates troops returning to Earth with a retrograde mod but the individual's changed genes remain. Discrimination against these soldiers is uncommon but it happens. Troops are regularly given passes to Liberty where they make use of the city's bars and other entertainment facilities. The current commander of the 30,000 troops at the fort is General Masazumi O'Dea though operation control is handled by his aide-de-camp, General Raymond Rechler. O'Dea is also responsible for operational control of all Space, Air and Navy (including Marine) forces in the American Arm.

Corporations and Foundations

All American institutions with colonial interests maintain an office in Liberty. International companies, or at least those not based in a US state or territory, often find themselves shut out of the local business climate but the persistent survive. The largest company operating within the city is AmeriCo and the TransNat's brand is found across Liberty County. The triggered direct holographic advertising of the Core is unacceptable by Liberty's preferred social mores but marketing efforts are common, ranging from simple animated hand bills to sponsorships of cultural events. AmeriCo runs a convenience food and beverage packaging plant in Liberty. The plant processes a large quantity of local grains in its products but a number of trade secret ingredients are imported from the Core. The plant is almost completely automated with only a few local hires on staff, serving in roles that are cheaper to fill with people than machines. Local processors complain that AmeriCo, under the guidance of AmeriCo Ellis Executive VP Cicily VanAllen, engages in unfair trade practices. These complaints are usually ignored as the TransNat has a great deal of influence in the governor's office. AmeriCo utilises its own subsidiary cargo maglev service to transport products across the planet.

Trilon Industries' American Arm division headquarters is located in Liberty but it maintains a larger physical presence on Boise. Personal electronics manufacturing and light engineering projects, such as vehicle assembly, are the local office's primary concerns. Recently the TransNat placed large amounts of resources and personnel into its exploration departments. This shift has included the construction of radio and optical observatories as well as probes. The 7.7 light year limit of stutterwarp technology has resulted in no new solar system discoveries in the American Arm for four decades. But many outpost planets have yet to be fully charted, let alone untouched worlds thought to be uninhabited. Speculators believe that Trilon is also backing a stutterwarp tug project but there is no evidence of this in the AC +48 1595 89 system. If such a project does exist, it is being treated with the highest security.

The mission statement of Comspace Enterprises of Newark, New Jersey sells the company as one of the leading 'colonial infrastructure development managers in human space.' Comspace was a member of the corporate cartel that backed the foundation of the Tanstaafl mining colony on Aurore. After the bankruptcy of two of the cartel's members, resulting in the dissolution of the cooperative project, and the American government's freeze of Comspace's assets, the company spent most of the 2260s restructuring. As of 2300, Comspace is a profitable company but has not regained its status as a TransNat. The local office in Liberty is responsible for much of the microwave communication and power transmission networks on Ellis. Comspace Enterprises is considering expanding its operations into the colony's Canadian and Nigerian enclaves.

Microtec, a technology and software application TransNat, is heavily lobbying Liberty city hall to adapt both an official Augmented Reality presence and a TrafCon infrastructure. Its attempts have met with heavy resistance by locals unwilling to entertain a surveillance culture. It has recently taken an interest in mining with its recent purchase and reorganisation of local employer, PetroEl. Ellis Consolidated Metals has launched a memetic attack campaign against Microtec, accusing it of 'Core world carpetbagging.' Microtec is also interested in military contracts. It recently upgraded Fort Patton's computer systems and is competing with Hyde Dynamics to develop a military cybernetics facility.

Other strong corporate presences in Liberty include vehicle designer Bridgeport Swift and firearms and machinery manufacturer the Rawlings Group of Texas.

The Alberta Farmers' Collective has been a close ally of the Ellis government since the colony's founding. AFC advisors work closely with the American Extrasolar Colonial Administration to ensure the most sound and profitable agricultural practices are used by all colonists. The Collective's Liberty office is a hands-on training centre for immigrants new to farming. It is also a research laboratory for new desert-climate resistant crop strains and hydrological extraction and recycling techniques. As the existing irrigation and aqueduct network is reaching its physical limit, AFC engineers have begun building radiative condenser farms and other aerial well structures around Liberty. This is considered by many to be a stop-gap solution and proposals for deep aquifer exploration and extraction are working their way through committees.

The American Interstellar Science Institute is an academic foundation dedicated to astronomy, physical cosmology, aerospace engineering and planetology. The AISI supports its research through survey expeditions to unexplored planets and by selling any valuable mineralogical information to private industry. The institute currently cooperates with an Australian group in the management of the Jovian planet research station on Gibbet's largest moon, Bucking. The institute's Liberty office is primarily used as a recruiting station for freelance explorers and as an administrative facility for its operations in the system.

The Pioneer Society, a new foundation, keeps an office in Liberty. The society was established in 2297 by William Stanton, a wealthy starship designer and pilot who made his fortune in a collaborative project with Trilon. The intention of the foundation is the private exploration of Ellis and other worlds in the American Arm. The group has received considerable blowback from the Australian-American Exploration Council. The AAEC believes that Stanton's proposals are too dangerous for a small and amateur group. Stanton has publicly countered that all of his efforts fall within AAEC guidelines and is inviting the Council to join him. Powerful private interest groups have publicly pressured the Council to release its public domain information to the Society.

Politics and Power

Liberty County is divided into twenty-five districts. Each district is granted a representative seated on the city-county council. The mayor and council members are elected to four year terms with no term limits. The council is responsible for budgets, taxation, financial appropriation for city operations, appointing commissioners and writing local laws. The Popular Conservatives hold a 56% majority of the council along with the mayor's office. The rest of the council are registered American party members and independents.

The Popular Conservatives' leadership in civic affairs is a reflection of the core beliefs of Liberty residents – a fundamentalist view of the Statement of Democratic Principles, the 24th century descendent of the original Bill of Rights, along with stability, prosperity and financial responsibility. The Popular Conservatives are also very friendly with powerful corporate interests. This has resulted in a small but growing backlash from voters. A strong populist belief considers corporate interests as intrusive as, if not more so than, government observation. With the election of the American party's Joseph Orsaluk to the national presidency, the mainstream political left has been growing across the American Arm. The Socialist party, with its belief in restrictive firearms laws, has been unable to pick up votes beyond its core base – intellectuals and labour groups – and has been limited in influence to college campuses.

Mayor Spencer Hart (PC) is in the middle of his second term. Born in Liberty, he was raised in the city and attended Ellis University before joining the Marine Corps. After twenty-three years of service and attaining a master's degree from Marine Corps University he retired as a Lieutenant Colonel and became self-employed as a business consultant. His distinguished service record and reputation as a 'self-made man' captured the respect of Liberty's population. Hart defeated the incumbent by ten percentage points. Controversy followed Hart's decision to privatise the county's water network but the profits from the sale to AmeriCo have been used to update much needed infrastructure and add new green spaces under the domes.

The Liberty City-County Council Minority Leader is Helen Katz (A). Katz was born in Fairview, a medium-sized town located north east of Liberty. After graduating from Ellis University's Reserve Officer Training Corps program and Armour Officer School, she served as a first lieutenant in the US Army's 11th ACR. Katz faced disciplinary action early in her career when she was accused of smuggling contraband on behalf of the local Sons of Liberty chapter. Katz was later cleared of the charge but the experience soured her on further military service. After resigning her commission she was hired by the Alberta Farmer's Collective as a human resources director. Katz won her first election while running in Liberty's 2nd district, promising to bring a progressive voice to county government. Katz is considered the senior-most American party member in Liberty and maintains a frosty relationship with her counterpart on the council, Majority Leader Ronald Wilkins.

Cicily VanAllen, AmeriCo's Ellis Division Executive Vice-President, is the leading voice in business affairs in Liberty. A veteran of the company, she was born in the borough of Manhattan on Earth. Her mother's second husband was an officer in one of AmeriCo's major subsidiaries. This nepotistic connection, combined with her own drive, landed VanAllen a management position after graduation from AmeriCo's Leadership College in the Metroplex. While the position on Ellis was far from VanAllen's ideal posting, she turned the division's lagging sales numbers around, seemingly through sheer force of will. She has led the Ellis division office for over a decade, though cosmetic and genetic alteration has kept her appearance at something resembling 30 years of age. She is a very public face for Liberty's business culture, often writing opinion pieces for the news media and appearing on interviews. She is married with a 20 year-old daughter though she keeps that side of her life away from prying eyes.

Personalities

Director Malcom Green

The United States Department of Extraplanetary Resources (USDER) is responsible for assigning land use and water rights to all American colonial citizens as well as enforcing resource management laws. On Ellis, where water usage is tightly controlled, the department can determine the economic success of local farms. The director of the Liberty office is Malcom Green. Born in Jamaica in 2247, Green's father, a distinguished cyberneticist, moved the family to Reston, Virginia when he took up a fellowship at Marymount University.

After receiving his law degree Green entered federal service. He was sent to Ellis by the Norman Isaacs administration to assist in transitioning Ellis to statehood. Moving his family to the colony in 2274, he became chief legal counsel to the AECA senior administrator. Through the 2280s he mediated land use conservation laws between the federal and state governments. In 2291, the Secretary of Extraplanetary Resources appointed him director of the Ellis Bureau of Resource Management.

Green not only leads an administrative office, he is in charge of a small task force of uniformed Rangers and plain clothes Special Agents who are responsible for preventing and investigating crimes on federal land.

Green is an Average Non-combatant NPC with the Dry World DNAM.

Meeting Green: The EBRM is responsible for areas of land all across Ellis. It is dangerous work and Green will always reach out to trustworthy characters with military or law enforcement backgrounds to assist in patrols or investigations of mining accidents. Characters with backgrounds in journalism or technical sciences may find Green a useful contact when studying American federal policy at work in the colonies.

NPC Motivation Results: *Spade 4:* Green is a career government bureaucrat who also happens to like his work. He has a reputation for fairness but his word is final. *Heart Jack:* As a lawyer and loyal agent of the American government, he strongly believes in the rule of law. Those who would cheat the system to gain an advantage anger him greatly.

Superintendent Billie-Lynn Braxton

The Ellis State Police have a two-fold mission: protect the infrastructure and employees of the Ellis government and patrol the unincorporated areas of the colony. The state police superintendent is Billie-Lynn Braxton. Born in 2235 on Ellis, Braxton was among the first children born to the planet's early settlers. She began her law enforcement career at age nineteen when she joined the AECA's small constabulary force, the Colonial Rangers, as a deputy. She rose through the ranks over the following twenty years eventually being appointed Chief of Community Affairs.

When the Ellis Colonial Rangers were folded into the newly formed Ellis State Police in 2276, Braxton and her fellow officers were brought into the command of the new governor's office. She was appointed Superintendent of State Police by the current governor in 2297. Braxton has been a part of two large group marriages and counts seven sister-wives and ten husbands, along with their 115 progeny, as part her immediate family.

Braxton is nearing retirement but is committed to seeing through her term. Her primary concerns are a lack of available resources to effectively patrol the colony and the rise of New America fanaticism in Ellis's farmlands. The 5,500 state troopers spread across the planet are spread too thin to provide effective security for the growing state population.

Braxton is an Experienced Non-combatant NPC with the Dry World DNAM.

Meeting Braxton: It is unlikely that characters will meet Braxton directly but one of her representatives in the recruitment office will reach out to characters with clean criminal records who are interested in either joining the force or contracting as a temporary deputy. Characters may also be contacted by political operatives opposing the current governor's office or news media producers who are looking to dig up dirt on the superintendent's efforts. Braxton may or may not be aware that a group of her detectives are on outside payrolls including AmeriCo, the local mob and even New America.

NPC Motivation Results: *Club Five:* While Braxton is now too old to get her hands dirty, in her youth she had no hesitation in applying physical force to belligerent suspects. She assigns her troopers a great deal of latitude in order to complete their assignments, including lethal methods if necessary. *Heart Ace:* Braxton believes in justice first and the rule of law second. She has little tolerance for politics and lawyers and has been known to bend or even quietly break the rules in order to apprehend a known criminal.

Zachariah Modine

Zachariah Modine is a Liberty County farmer and rancher and a 32nd-Tier planner in New America. Born on Ellis in 2250, he spent his childhood and teens as a farm labourer. He enlisted in the Marines at age 18 in order to escape what he felt was a life of repetitive drudgery. It was while he was in the Corps that he met Nathan Harris, an armour specialist and member of New America. Harris took the young Modine under his wing, sharing with him the writings of New America's founder, Carl Hughes. When Harris was shot and killed during an altercation with military police, Modine carried on his work.

Modine rose to the rank of Staff Sergeant while recruiting others into the group. He declined to sign another contract term of service when he suspected the authorities were getting too close and he returned to civilian life on the family farm. At the age of 32 he took control of the farm's business operations when his father died. He used his connections to begin quietly assembling a group of like-minded farmers who worried about the growing government and corporate interests that would come with Ellis's statehood. Modine appointed himself and the group as Liberty's New Aristocracy, the planners and policy makers for the local New America.

Modine has spent twenty-five years building various New America cells and caching weapons and supplies for the time when full-on revolution will come to the colony. In homage to Carl Hughes, Modine has written a series of documents known as the *Codex Libertas*, instructions for Liberty area cell leaders in the event of armed conflict.

Local and federal law enforcement has kept watch on Modine for years. However he has been careful to keep his activities quiet and avoids breaking any local statutes. He only keeps contact with those he trusts implicitly and weeds out troublemakers and those who would bring outside attention.

Modine is an Experienced Combatant NPC with the Dry World DNAM.

Meeting Modine: Modine will not contact characters directly but one of his agents may ask less scrupulous player characters to run what seem like innocuous errands, such as transporting fuel. Outside interests, such as a corporate security office or even the media, may pay the characters to infiltrate a New America cell in order to gain access to Modine's inner circle.

NPC Motivation Results: *Club Jack:* While privacy rights are becoming more of an issue on Ellis, Modine's xenophobia manifests itself in a rage and narcissism-fuelled fanaticism. *Heart Nine:* Modine knows exactly which strings to pull in order to get what he wants.

Jürgen Beck

Jürgen Beck is the boss of the local Freihafen Black Hand syndicate in Liberty. Born in 2258 in Ceske Vary on Tirane, he had a reputation as an antisocial youth and caught the attention of local syndicate 'made men.' He served in the Freihafen army for two years as a mess cook and reached the rank of *obergefreiter* before his honourable discharge. Beck became a soldier in the Lange organised crime family and by the age of 29 he was a made man. He was heavily involved in loan-sharking, racketeering and illegal gambling.

During a case of mistaken identity, Beck murdered Kerstin Weisz, sister of Lange family soldier and suspected law enforcement informant, Sarah Weisz. While Beck was cleared of wrong doing by the family boss, he was considered a liability in the syndicate. Declared persona non grata on Tirane, Beck fled to Ellis in 2291 with a hand-picked group of associates from his street gang days and a large bank account.

Liberty's small population and more libertarian attitude regarding traditional vices pushed Beck into investing in local construction and maintenance companies. With his earnings he started up his own company, Beck General Contracting, which he used to launder funds from his primary source of income, smuggling. Local AmeriCo-affiliated mafia bosses use Beck's syndicate as contract labour for various illicit enterprises. Beck is currently feuding with mob boss Nicky Bruno but local syndicate captains, with AmeriCo's blessings, are negotiating a truce.

Beck is an Average Combatant NPC.

Meeting Beck: Less than scrupulous or desperate characters may be contracted by Beck to engage in various illegal operations such as smuggling weapons, stealing trade secrets from AmeriCo rivals or even engaging in violent actions. For law-abiding characters, Beck is a juicy target for law enforcement and characters may be hired by local law enforcement to help gather evidence against his organisation.

NPC Motivation Results: *Diamond 6:* Beck considers himself a businessman and runs his syndicate like a company. He will always haggle and push for the best return on investment. *Clubs 9:* Beck is quick to violence but unlike many mobsters, he does not relish in it. He does not believe in torture and avoids harming 'civilians' but will use intimidation and even murder to accomplish a goal.

New America

Twilight Era

The origins of the New America movement can be found in the decades prior to the Twilight Era. Carl Hughes, a former United States military officer, was heir to a media mogul's fortune. Hughes had resigned his commission over what he regarded as the United States' practice of 'appeasement' toward the world's greatest threats, communism and socialism. With access to finances he turned to politics and attempted an independent run at national office. Hughes's unpolished style led to his sound defeat by opposition candidates. After convictions for tax-evasion and campaign finance mismanagement he spent eight months in Federal prison.

After his release, Hughes returned to politics and used his money to establish a political action committee. Hughes advertised his group, New America, as upholders of traditional conservative values. In reality it promoted an ideology of reactionary fundamentalism. When the Christian conservative movement declined his backing, Hughes founded his own radical church which served as a tax-shelter for his political and economic activities. He forged alliances with anti-government survivalists and racist religious groups, published crack-pot revisionist historical tracts, and screened new church members – typically wealthy, influential or politically savvy individuals and families obsessed with eschatological theology. New America remained a small and low-key operation which allowed it to avoid the interest of American law enforcement. Just prior to the Twilight Era, Hughes retired to his estate headquarters in the Shenandoah Mountains of Virginia where he wrote about his philosophies of a traditional America, one based on his own religious and political philosophies rather than Constitutional principles.

While Hughes was in his retirement, the leadership of New America, known as the Core Committee, remained vigilant. Before the destruction of the Twilight Era, New America stockpiled weapons and supplies, purchased failing farms and small towns, and established operational cells across North America including Canada, swelling its numbers to over 300,000.

During the Twilight Era, New America sprang into action as municipalities struggled with the breakdown of civil services. Spotty historical records indicate that New American revolutionaries had infiltrated several local governments including that of Arkansas and Florida. New America cells operating in the South even utilised stolen airships to drop explosives on unsuspecting towns. Concentration camps were set up outside of captured areas where the 'genetically undesirable' were interred as slave labourers. The remaining locals were placed under the eye of New America garrison troops and those with needed technical skills were simply taken. Resistance was met with immediate execution.

After two decades fighting, the split in the American government was reconciled at the Conference of Memphis. The defeat of New America became the new government's top priority. Unable to hold territory against the overwhelming might of the reformed military, the majority of New America's leadership was captured, killed or scattered. Those members of the Core Committee that the United States was able to imprison were tried by a military court. All were found guilty of a long list of war crimes and human rights violations and were executed. Those who escaped either fled the country or changed their identities and disappeared into the shattered wastelands of the nation.

The 22nd Century

America's fractured leadership and broken infrastructure allowed an expansionist Mexico to take control of the American Southwest. At the height of the Twilight Era, Mexican troops held Texas, New Mexico, Arizona and southern California. By the time of the American federal government's reconciliation these regions were fully integrated into Mexico proper.

In 2099, Texan separatists launched a strike against the Mexican military, kicking off five years of open American-Mexican warfare. The Peace of El Paso officially ended the war in 2103 and ensured Texan independence but the United States continued to fund separatist causes in its other former states. This included sending deniable Special Forces units to train local militias.

After the Battle of Los Angeles in 2106, the Mexican Civil War drew to a close. Several American Green Berets were captured by Mexican forces when the city fell to amphibious invasion. The United States officially denied involvement. Rather than being sent to a POW camp, the Green Berets were incarcerated at Punta Prieta in the state of Baja.

Among those captured was 23 year-old Army Sgt. Rutherford Ulysses Latour. Latour's father was a political refugee who had fled persecution in southern California. Born in Oakland, Rutherford Latour left his college medical program for military service. During the time of his imprisonment, he and his fellow Anglo-American inmates formed a prison gang called New America. Latour was familiar with Carl Hughes's *American Manifesto* and chose the name to spite both the Mexicans and the United States government, which the prisoners considered having abandoned them.

In 2115, a progressive-leftist bloc took control of Mexico. As one of several acts of appeasement with the United States, it released dozens of American prisoners. Latour settled in Arkansas where he wrote a prospectus for a reformed New America entitled *Prescripts of an American*. The essay was both a scathing critique of the new federal government and a racist tract indicting a 'Hispanic conspiracy to undermine American sovereignty.' The essay found traction in a region that had been economically stymied during the Twilight Era. The former New America prison gang evolved into a political force with an active military wing known as the Knights.

Through 2123, New America claimed responsibility for a series of terror attacks across Florida, the Texarkana region, California and Arizona. This included the destruction of a passenger train at the US-Texas border, the bombing of a Texas Marine Corps barracks in Corpus Christi and a Hispanic congregation in Miami and a mass shooting at a shopping mall in San Diego. Meanwhile, New America supporters won several local elections in the southern United States.

By 2127, a cooperative US-Texas counter-terrorist effort began to capture or eliminate most active New America cells. Latour fled to the Cayman Islands where he continued to coordinate the organisation's political wing. In January 2128 he was found dead in his hotel room, the apparent victim of a gunshot wound to the head. Mexican naval commandos were later attributed to the assassination. New America's terror operations in North and Central America soon ceased though its political operatives remained in place for decades.

The 23rd Century & Beyond

The third wave of New America formed as a reaction to a growing culture of surveillance and the expanding welfare state. The Shroud adhocracy was a popular anti-surveillance group that promoted a strong cryptosurvivalist mentality. Thomas Price and Marc Duke were wealthy Freelancers, as well as members of the Shroud, who shared a passion for history and a distaste for progressive policies that disincentivised individual initiative.

In 2219, Price published a controversial political screed entitled *What Happened to America?* which advocated the violent overthrow of the American government. The piece was panned by critics. When the adhocracy successfully voted to remove Price from its closed membership, Duke, a supporter, left the adhocracy in protest.

Duke was a successful informatics specialist and part of a community of like-minded anti-government technocrats. Price was a memetic engineer with years of experience in programming beliefs. He was also an expert in authoritarian beliefs, especially those of Carl Hughes. Duke and Price pooled their respective resources to form the Minuteman Trust Association, a business that would manage a New America secret society.

While Duke used his connections to recruit more wealthy benefactors, Price crafted a new memetic movement. Known as Ascendancism, the meme was a heavily disguised reintroduction of Carl Hughes' various philosophies: a Natural Aristocracy of the wealthy and privileged is necessary for the betterment of mankind and a one-person, one-vote method of democracy is inherently flawed as it allowed the uneducated, the emotional and the undedicated an equal voice in policy making. Ascendancism deliberately avoided the racist rhetoric of previous New American movements but the meme purposefully condemned regions of the country with socially inclusive and egalitarian cultures.

Within three years, New America had recruited 4000 contributing members, primarily anti-globalisation Freelancers. With its base secure, the group began lobbying conservative politicians, primarily in the South. By 2225, New America was making major financial contributions to pro-isolationist lawmakers and publishing policy papers.

With a financial and security system in place, Duke secretly organised a paramilitary cell which served as New America's security force, shock troops and personal bully boys. Dubbed 'Red Shirts' by the media, after the 19th-century Southern paramilitaries, they were responsible for assaults on corporate and government VIPs, the bombings of regional public assistance centres and a Trilon office and sparking an anti-government riot in Atlanta. Law enforcement considered the Red Shirts an independent terrorist organisation until a National Security Office Memetic Response Unit linked the group with Ascendancism and New America. Duke, Price and other members of New America where subject to conspiracy and treason charges. After a six day armed standoff at Price's farm outside Atlanta, Duke and Price committed suicide. Many New America members received lengthy prison sentences or mind wipes.

In 2300, New America groups exist in isolated pockets in the South and the Midwest but there is no co-ordinated movement. The average American citizen considers New America to be the radical fringe and most Southerners regard them as an embarrassment. Like the Ku Klux Klan of the late 20th century,

New America in the Core consists of small disorganised cells with a total membership of less than 4000. However, on the edge of the American Arm, New America is quickly growing.

The majority of colonists selected for the first wave of off-world immigration to Ellis were from Western and Plains regions of America and Canada. Many of those that qualified held private pro-New America sympathies. Upon arrival, these colonists discovered that the isolation and lack of government oversight was fertile ground for a new and stronger version of New America. Estimates of sympathisers on Ellis ranges from 300,000 to 500,000 but active membership is less than 125,000.

Organisation and Philosophy

New America's structure is based on Carl Hughes's original cell concept which was borrowed from secret societies and revolutionary groups. Only the top echelons of New America know all the leaders of local cells and cell leaders are only aware of no more than two other cells.

The group utilises numbers to designate rank, with higher numbers, or 'Tiers' outranking lower numbers. All new members start at 1st-Tier which equals a low-level soldier. Length of service will automatically promote members up to 12th-Tier. Members are promoted into 13th-Tier and up to 30th-Tier by merit and time. Cell leaders fall within these tiers along with mission planners, security specialists, quartermasters and recruiters. Starting at the 31st-Tier are what Carl Hughes referred to as the 'Natural Aristocracy,' the small handful of executives responsible for the overall mission of New America. The 40th-Tier is New America's senior-most executive but the identity of this individual, or whether the role is even held, is unknown at this time.

Those at and below the 30th-Tier are considered 'Citizens' and their rights, including marriage, are only approved by the Natural Aristocracy. Below the Citizens are 'Seconds' and 'Thirds,' those without rights but still a part of the State. At the bottom are those without tier ranking, known as Long Contract labourers. The LCs are considered wards of the state but are in reality a slave pool. As of 2300, no actual LCs exist.

Various cells are organised to handle different tasks ranging from procurement, recruitment, PR, management and security. Security groups are the hard core paramilitaries and typically consist of former mercenaries and military personnel. Their training camps serve as screening and recruitment centres.

The New America of 2300 has adopted Carl Hughes's *American Manifesto* as its guiding principle but the interpretation of the work has evolved over time. Hughes's cult-like religious belief emphasised the 'natural and inherent superiority' of whites, especially northern Europeans, over all other humans. Link technology and the egalitarian monoculture of the Core has almost thoroughly discredited most racist views. However, New America has become attached to the notion that, while skin colour does not determine superiority, there are those who are worthy of rights and those who are not. At its core, New America believes that all aspects of life – the economy, morality, science and the wards of the state – must be rigidly controlled. The economy must be controlled to keep the populace employed, morality must be controlled to keep the general populace in line, science must be controlled to prevent the population from self-destructing, women must be controlled to keep the family together and a controlled labour class must exist so that its betters can focus their energies on more important tasks.

The National Security Office

Established in 2198, the National Security Office is the direct progeny of the former Federal Bureau of Investigation. It is an agency of the US Department of Justice (DoJ) and the NSO Director reports directly to the US Attorney General (USAG). The NSO was preceded by the Justice Department's Criminal Investigation Bureau, various military investigation divisions and other sister agencies until their merger by Congress. Conservatives raised warnings regarding the dangers of a national police force but the desire for greater government efficiency and reduced tax burdens swayed public opinion.

Headquartered in Virginia, the NSO maintains a field office in every major city and state capital along with satellite resident agencies across the Core and the American Arm. Field offices are supervised by a Special Agent-in-Charge (SAC) and a small team of Assistant SACs (ASACs). Resident agencies are supervised by a Senior Resident Agent (SRA). Larger offices feature an in-house Supervisory Special Agent (SSA) who oversees day-to-day operations. All offices have teams of Special Agents (SAs) who engage in field work, a Tactical Unit for critical response and a team of support staff employees. Support staff are typically in-house scientists, motor pool/ hardsuit technicians and informatics specialists. The NSO provides attachés to all American diplomatic missions.

All New Agent Trainees are processed through a 20-week training program at the Federal Law Enforcement Academy at Marine Corps Base Quantico in Virginia or the satellite campus in Georgia. NSO SWAT Special Agents are provided an additional six months of fieldcraft and marksmanship training with the USMC. Quantico is also home to the NSO's Forensic Technology Centre (FTC), America's premiere criminal science lab, and the Georgia campus also serves as an international law enforcement academy for investigators from allied nations. It is not unusual to find agents from the British Commonwealth attending classes with their American counterparts.

Working in conjunction with the FTC is the NSO's Office of Data Management (ODM) based in West Virginia. The ODM is home to the NSO's record keeping efforts and is the operational centre for the United States government's national surveillance system. Human technicians and digital 'bots sort and file millions of hours of video surveillance footage, Link activity files and audio recordings along with criminal biometric data. In order to protect the civil rights of American citizens, the ODM is forbidden by law to share data information with the military or the American Intelligence Service. However, privacy advocates have long suspected the ODM of skirting the law through legal technicalities.

The National Security Office is divided into five operational branches, the two largest of which represent the agency's core responsibility – Criminal Investigation, the branch responsible for law enforcement, and Intelligence Services, the branch responsible for domestic surveillance, counterintelligence and counter-terrorism. In recent years, the Intelligence Services branch has been successful in blocking German *Bundesnachrichtendienst* (BND) efforts to infiltrate American interests. The three other branches are Human Resources, Information and Equipment Technology and Science Services (forensics and medical examination).

While the agency maintains tactical response units trained in aggressive hostage rescue/counter-terrorism tactics, the business dress-attired Special Agents are the most recognisable NSO employees in the public consciousness. They are afforded both investigative and arrest powers by the US federal government and are responsible for the enforcement of all federal laws along with combating domestic terrorism and violent crime. The NSO becomes involved when a) it is contacted by a state or municipal police department regarding crimes that cross jurisdictional lines or that exceed the resources of local law enforcement, b) a crime occurs on Federal property including military bases or c) a crime occurs against a US citizen in foreign territory.

The NSO maintains a field office in Liberty on Ellis as well as resident agencies in all municipalities across the colony. Forty agents are assigned to Ellis along with 95 professional support personnel. The entirety of Ellis along with several orbital assets fall within the jurisdiction of the local NSO field office. As a result it is perpetually understaffed. The electronic and remote surveillance methods used on Earth are considered taboo on Ellis, thus successful NSO investigations require a great deal of human manpower. The lack of surveillance also encourages smuggling and other illicit activities and so the field office always has a full caseload.

Garnering employment as a National Security Office agent is a very competitive process. Compensation is high for a government employee and the turnover rate is very low. Only highly qualified candidates are considered, typically those with intensive secondary educations or a strong service record at the local law enforcement level. However, the difficulty of acquiring resources from Earth combined with small local populations have forced colonial field offices to become creative when hiring new assets. The NSO directorate has authorised colonial Special-Agents-in-Charge to directly recruit new agents from local populations. Colonial recruits are required to be American citizens with either a military or law enforcement background, to pass a government service exam and to have no criminal history. These agent trainees receive a special waiver which by-passes the NSO Academy but mandates a three-month accelerated training program which covers criminology, forensic science and Federal law. Upon completion, these agents are assigned the rank of Special Agent (Adjunct). While adjunct agents are placed in a lower pay-tier and are subordinate to full agents, they are provided the same arrest and investigative authority as their colleagues.

Surveillance on Ellis

Outside of undeveloped nations, surveillance is a constant in the Core. The average pedestrian in a major city is continuously hit with targeted advertising and reactions are recorded on behalf of marketing specialists. Stationary and drone mounted security cameras record vehicle and foot traffic and monitor for seditious and criminal activity.

The colonies are very different in this regard. Many colonists born on Earth left the Core to escape the constant electronic intrusion in their lives. And as the population density of an average colonial settlements is a fraction of that of a Core city, effective commercial and government surveillance is both cost-prohibitive and ineffective. As a result, settlements operate without the usual electronic barrage. Advertisements, if they exist at all, range from simple animation loops playing on spray-on LED covered surfaces to old-fashioned handbills printed on paper. Security cameras are typically limited to travel hubs and government buildings.

From a law enforcement perspective, a low-tech culture requires police on Ellis to engage in traditional practices when investigating a crime. Cultivating a network of informants, good forensic science, keen observation and a logical mind are requirements for police working in colonial environments.

Liberty Field Office

The NSO's Liberty Field Office is headed by SAC Elena Jiménez, ASACs John Nieten and David Kirk and SSA Karli Kapinos.

Frontier Justice

Compared to their local counterparts, federal agencies in the Core have the most-current technology and a deep well of resources from which to draw upon. On Ellis, the distinction between the NSO, the Ellis State Police and municipal police is simply one of jurisdiction. Like their local counterparts, Ellis-based Special Agents are trained in multiple disciplines and should expect to be assigned to multiple cases across the planet.

While all Special Agents are full-time government employees, dedicated crime scene investigators and other specialised support personnel do not exist on Ellis. Field office motor pool employees, lab technicians and IT staff are civilians who often work multiple contracts. Therefore, when assigning Special Agents to Ellis, NSO managers look for ideal recruits with diverse skill sets ranging from medicine, criminology, academic and even military backgrounds. To their credit, Special Agents have access to better equipment than local police. They are also demonstrably less likely to fall victim to corruption.

Ellis NSO agents are expected to be stronger, smarter and more capable than their Core brethren. Often compared to a more cerebral Texas Ranger, many Ellis-based NSO agents carry this burden as a badge of honour.

Special Agent-in-Charge Elena Jiménez

Elena Jiménez is the head of the NSO's Liberty field office. Born in 2248 in Maryland on Earth, Jiménez studied international relations at Georgetown University and received a Juris Doctor from the University of Virginia School of Law in 2272. She was considered an exceptionally promising candidate by several recruiters and was hired by the Department of Justice as an Assistant United States Attorney (AUSA).

While serving as a senior litigator in the Reston, Virginia AG Office, Jiménez oversaw the prosecution of cases involving fraud and accounting malpractice in the corporate world. Jiménez successfully landed a guilty verdict against the CEO and CFO of Kretch Minerals, Ltd. for stock manipulation when the two falsified reports of a heavy tantalum strike on Hermes. She joined the NSO as a Special Agent in 2285 where she served in the US embassy in Toronto and became the chief legal adviser to the Boston field office in 2291. While expressing a desire to stay in the Core, the Liberty field office SAC was scheduled to retire and in 2296 she relocated to the colonies to further her career.

Jiménez's assumption of the SAC post was a source of friction inside the Liberty office. Considered an 'outsider' who did not understand Ellis's rural culture, she further alienated herself by refusing DNA modification. To natives and long-time agents assigned to the colony, this was a strong indication that Jiménez was not interested in committing to the job but rather in climbing through the ranks of the NSO bureaucracy. She

redeemed herself in the eyes of her subordinates when she led a successful investigation into the 2297 bombing of the Marine Corps barracks on Carlton. Months later, Provolution cell leader Marvin Digiacomo and two associates were prosecuted and convicted thanks to the evidence and prosecutorial guidance provided by Jiménez and the Liberty field office.

Jiménez has a reputation for being emotionally cold and somewhat lacking in social graces. She makes up for this with a keen analytical mind and an amazing grasp of procedure, government and the law. She relies on her ASACs to be personable faces of the Liberty office's leadership team.

SAC Elena Jiménez is an Elite Non-combatant NPC.

NPC Motivation Results: *Heart 5:* Rather than patriotism, Jiménez is driven by a need for personal accomplishment. *Spade Jack:* While a professional, Jiménez is often frustrated by the lack of access to Core world surveillance technology and her perception of an uncooperative colonial population.

Assistant Special Agent-in-Charge John Nieten

John Nieten is one of two ASACs reporting to Elena Jiménez. Nieten's primary responsibility is to manage the field office's tactical element and oversee training. Born in 2259 on Ellis, he fits the mould of the stereotypical shaved-headed spit-and-polish SWAT commander. Nieten attended a prestigious preparatory school prior to enlisting in the Marines at age 18. He joined the NSO after a two terms of service in the military and after two years as a Special Agent graduated from the SWAT Training Program at Quantico. Jiménez relies on Nieten for all paramilitary actions the field office may undertake and to act as a liaison with the local military presence.

ASAC John Nieten is an Experienced Combatant NPC with the Dry World DNAM.

NPC Motivation Results: *Club 8:* Nieten is very aggressive and accepts violence as a method for solving problems. *Heart 3:* He strongly believes in the importance of the chain of command and follows orders without question.

Assistant Special Agent-in-Charge David Kirk

David Kirk is Elena Jiménez's second ASAC. Kirk's specialty is in administration, business affairs and public relations. Born in 2263 to an Ellis-based petrochemical magnate, Kirk was groomed to take over the company by his mother. However, after graduating from the University of Nanton with a degree in Criminology, he chose to enter government service instead. As a field agent he was responsible for the arrest of the Link-based evangelist Greg Hale on charges of fraud and distribution of copyrighted intellectual property. The arrest came during a period of low public opinion of the NSO and Kirk's interactions with the media helped to greatly sway that judgement to the positive. While Kirk is a brother-husband in a joint marriage, he is naturally handsome and charismatic and is not above using both looks and charm to sway opinion in his favour.

ASAC David Kirk is an Experienced Non-combatant NPC with the Dry World DNAM.

NPC Motivation Results: *Spade Ace:* Kirk would be as at home in a corporate board room as he is in the government. People naturally like him and SAC Jiménez uses him as a mouthpiece with the public and the media. *Club 3:* Kirk is not easily intimidated.

Supervisory Special Agent Karli Kapinos

Karli Kapinos is the Liberty field office SSA. Her responsibility is to oversee the daily case load of all Special Agents assigned to the Liberty office. Born in 2263, she joined Liberty's local police department as a detective after graduating from Garfield Community University with a degree in Forensic Psychology. Beginning her career in the Robbery Unit she eventually moved to Narcotics. Fast-tracked to becoming one of the youngest lieutenants in the department's short history, she instead applied to and was accepted by the NSO Academy. Her police experience qualified her for quick advancement and in 2299 she was appointed SSA by Elena Jiménez. Kapinos's role in the field office is similar to that of a captain in smaller police departments. All Special Agents assigned to criminal investigations report to her on a regular basis.

SSA Karli Kapinos is an Experienced Non-combatant NPC with the Dry World DNAM.

NPC Motivation Results: *Diamond 3:* Kapinos is more pragmatic than patriotic and use employment in the NSO, with its generous compensation, a means to a personal end. *Spade King:* Kapinos has a two-year-old son, the father of whom she keeps a closely guarded secret.

Player Character NSO Agents

As agents of the National Security Office and the American government, player characters should expect stringent rules regarding their behaviour and choices of action; more so than Freelancers such as mercenaries and troubleshooter. Agents are expected to not only enforce all federal laws but to hold themselves to a respectable code of behaviour. This is important to maintain public trust in the government. Government agents also have access to more resources than a freelancer, which reduces the amount of physical risk a character should be expected to engage in.

2300AD referees interested in maintaining setting verisimilitude in their law enforcement campaign should work directly with all players during character creation. Rogue career paths and foreign citizenship are discouraged unless an extenuating circumstance is presented. For example, a character who worked deep undercover in a crime family would be an acceptable career path.

Expectations and Tools of Law Enforcement

The information provided is by no means exhaustive but is a good resource for players unfamiliar with law enforcement techniques or who are stuck for ideas on how to proceed in an adventure.

Evidence Accumulation

Law enforcement agents are expected to provide sufficient evidence of criminal activity to convict the accused in a federal court. If an arrested defendant is convicted or submits a guilty plea, the case is a success. If the defendant is found not guilty, all the case work the agent conducted along with the agent herself is considered tainted. Therefore it is the responsibility of every agent to identify and provide admissible evidence for a federal prosecutor to use in a case.

Submitted evidence must accomplish two goals – prove that a crime happened and link the defendant to the crime. Gathering this evidence happens in two ways – recovering it at a crime scene or obtaining it through the use of a *search warrant*. Unless there is corroborating physical evidence, criminal confessions are rarely, if ever, useful in a trial as a skilled defence attorney will claim the confession was obtained through coercion. Therefore evidence is primarily in the form of recovered objects, records, scientific analysis and surveillance data. Memetic assault and psychological tricks have rendered unsupported verbal courtroom testimony unreliable in 2300. To counter this, voluntary witness cortex hacking is used in support of cases but a witness must be present in court to testify that the cortex scan is truthful.

Search Warrants

As unreasonable searches and seizures are forbidden under the Statement of Democratic Principles, the search warrant is one of an agent's most powerful tools for evidence recovery. However, an agent must show *probable cause* in order to receive one from a federal judge. In order to prove probable cause, an agent must receive reliable testimony or documented hearsay (surveillance footage or recorded conversation). Search warrants are only necessary for examining private property. Open fields, abandoned structures or public areas do not require warrants. Transnational corporations in good standing are considered foreign territory and are not required to submit to search warrants though some will in order to maintain good public relations.

Properly filing an affidavit requires an agent to submit a complicated legal form, requiring a successful Admin, Edu, 2 hours, Average (+0) check. This time includes writing the submission along with review and approval by a judge. If the agent is rushed for time, the task requires a successful Admin, Edu, 1 hour, Difficult (-2) check or a successful Admin, Edu, 30 min, Very Difficult (-4) check. Failed attempts suffer penalties per the Task Chain DM rules. No agent may attempt this check more than 3 times per warrant request. Warrants are valid for 1D days.

Warrantless searches are applicable when the person in control of a piece of evidence relinquishes it, if a suspect is fleeing, in an emergency, if a piece of evidence faces destruction or if it is incidental to a suspect's arrest.

If a warrantless search is used, the arresting agent must make a successful Advocate, Edu, Routine (+2) check to a supervisor to explain the situation. If a check fails and the evidence owner requests its return, it must be relinquished.

Remote Surveillance and Electronic Surveillance

The American government differentiates remote surveillance and electronic surveillance. As the name implies, remote surveillance is observation done from a distance from a subject. Remote surveillance is a constant in the Core be it from targeted advertising biometric triggers, drone traffic cameras and even observation satellites. Any activity conducted in a public place or outside of a private domicile, such as a street or even a front yard, can be recorded legally. Criminals will often use electronic scramblers to conceal themselves from public observation but trained Special Agents can often counter this with old fashioned techniques, such as on-the-fly body posture analysis or even lip reading through binoculars. An opposed Recon, Int vs. Deception, Dex skill check can be used to determine if a Special Agent understands the general intention or ideas conveyed in a distant conversation.

Electronic surveillance is used to directly record active conversations and electronic records, such as real time monitoring of a Link profile. This surveillance can be conducted using, for example, shotgun microphones, hidden cameras, computer taps and even drones equipped with laser microphones and image recorders. Only law enforcement officials can submit evidence into record if gathered in this way and only through the use of a court ordered electronic surveillance warrant. While transnational corporations have the legal right to bug employees' company-owned homes, evidence gathered by a private security team is only admissible in a corporate court. Obtaining an electronic surveillance warrant requires the same process as a general search warrant. A Remote Operations, Dex check may be called for to keep a spy drone on target. Weather conditions and lighting will affect the check's difficulty.

Databases & the Link

The NSO's Office of Data Management maintains the largest criminal record and surveillance database in the United States. Agents posted to colony worlds face some issues utilising it as updates to local servers only occur when a starship that has recently visited the Core arrives. Colonial databases may lag days, weeks or even months behind. However, criminals who have arrived from the Core typically have records that stretch back months or even years. Even out-of-date records are good starting points for investigating agents. Local criminal databases tend to be more up-to-date in the colonies than federal systems so municipal, state and federal agencies often partner.

Criminal databases are not the only sources of information on suspects. On the federal level, the Internal Revenue Service (IRS), the Interstate Commerce Commission, which licenses not only ground based national transport workers but American commercial starship pilots, and public welfare bureaus are excellent sources of information. At the local level, licensing boards, motor vehicle bureaus and local tax departments are good sources.

Non-government databases, including unions and local businesses, are accessible only through a warrant.

The American government utilises a standard format for their records. Special Agents utilising these databases which will make a Simple (+6) Admin or Informatics, Edu check for general information such as personnel records, case files or licensing information. When investigating government financial records, a Simple (+6) Broker, Int check is used. Criminal records will include biometrics recorded at time of arrest, immediate family contact information, residential address and other relevant data including known associates. Non-criminal records will only include a basic image, government identification number and contact information including residential address.

Private databases are typically customised to meet the business or personal needs of the database owner. Warrant-holding Special Agents will make an Average (+0) Admin or Informatics, Edu check for general records and an Average (+0) Broker, Edu check for financial information. If a Special Agent is attempting to identify user information, such as the last individual to update a record, this will require an Average (+0) or Difficult (-2) Computers or Informatics, Int check. Unless a private database owner is attempting to mislead law enforcement, these databases will only contain information relevant to the company or owner. For example, a corporate database would only contain pertinent information to its operations – contracts, employee records, R&D histories and the like. Personal databases usually contain information on personal projects, hobbies and contacts lists.

Public databases are free to access to anyone. These typically utilise a simple algorithms that can check listings on the user's behalf without a skill check. However, if a Special Agent is conducting a much more in-depth search, a relevant skill check may be required. For example, Advocate would be used to search for a judicial ruling or a general Engineer check for information on specific starship designs.

If a Special Agent is broadening a search to the public Link, the process becomes what is known as data mining. If looking for past incidents related to a criminal suspect, the task is an Informatics EDU or INT skill check. The time and difficulty of the check depends on how successful a suspect has managed to stay out of the public eye or way from biometric sensors. For example, a performance artist engaged in civil disobedience would rate a Simple (+6) DM whereas a professional assassin would require a Formidable (-6) task check. An Exceptional Failure (-6 or less) results in the Special Agent latching onto false information and wasting time in a false pursuit. A referee and player may choose to roleplay the wasted effort or a referee may simply apply a time delay penalty.

Confidential Informants

A strong informant network is an excellent tool for law enforcement agents. Informants are typically the initial source of contact for information regarding criminal activity in an area or known suspects. Informants are motivated by a fear of arrest, assuming they are engaged or have been engaged in petty criminal activities, financial benefit and/or simple honesty/civic duty. Typical informants work alone and in service industries which expose them to a great deal of local rumour-mongering. These individuals include prostitutes, journalists, investigators, vehicle drivers, night-shift managers, ex-criminals, attendants, bartenders and private security guards.

Federal records of confidential informants are limited to code names or random number strings to ensure an informant's safety.

A player character can develop an NPC into a confidential informant in three ways:

- Contacts, allies and even rivals or enemies gained during character creation.
- Good roleplaying.
- Task checks utilising the Carouse, Persuade and Broker SOC skills. It is suggested that referees require a Task Chain over a series of hours or days in order to simulate the slow process of recruiting an informant and testing the provided information for reliability.

Evidence Processing for Vice and Violent Crime Investigations

The NSO investigates a variety of crimes but the two most common are violent crimes, specifically multiple murders, and vice trafficking which includes prostitution, narcotics, and banned or controlled substances and personal technologies.

Vice

Successful vice investigations typically involve determining the source of supply through undercover investigations, surveillance, informants and direct buys. If making a direct buy, an agent will need to make several buys and collect money used for purchasing, which becomes evidence. Money and financial records are used to show links between known and unknown vice traffickers in order to show conspiracy. Informants can also be used to make vice purchases so long as they are under constant surveillance and the threat of physical danger is minimal.

Vice products entered into evidence must show the following:

- Chain of custody is monitored and minimalised by the investigating agent.
- The agent did not come into unprotected contact with the object or substance.
- The object or substance was held in a sealed and secured container.
- The object or substance did not leave the evidence lock-up except for laboratory testing.

Agents will also be expected to provide surveillance footage of an arrest site. Fingerprints and other biometric data may be gathered at the site by crime scene investigators as supplemental evidence.

Field testing of a substance or object is only conducted by an agent prior to an arrest. Field testing is not admissible as evidence but is enough to confirm the presence of contraband and to arrest a suspect. An Easy (+4) Physical Sciences (chemistry), Edu check with a basic sampling kit (see *2300AD*, pg. 137) will confirm a chemical substance. An Easy (+4) Computers, Edu check with a forensics kit (see *Tools for Frontier Living*, pg. 99) will confirm illegal software.

Violent Crimes

Local law enforcement agencies are set up to handle homicide investigations but the NSO is called in when the scope of an investigation exceeds the capacity or jurisdiction of a municipal or state police department. Typically the NSO investigates the following types of violent crimes:

- Linked assaults or murders across various jurisdictions.
- Assaults or murders involving organised crime families.

- Kidnappings.
- Murders outside a state's jurisdiction, such as federal reserves and other special territories.
- Mass or attempted mass killings.

In the Core, NSO agents do not process a fresh crime scene directly. Scene analysis is handled initially by local resources and then NSO CSI teams. Only after all biometric and other physical evidence is secured is a scene opened to physical investigation by a team of NSO agents. Crime scene evidence is provided to the agents by the CSI team and the agents work with a coroner to determine the cause of death. However, in the colonies, agents often process crime scenes themselves.

Assuming that the death was not by natural or accidental causes and was not justifiable homicide, the coroner report becomes part of a criminal homicide investigation. All evidence is supplied to a federal prosecutor who determines which federal criminal homicide statue to prosecute under. Criminal homicides can fall under various murder and manslaughter laws.

Investigative methodology has changed little since Pre-Twilight. It is important, though not necessary for a conviction, to establish a suspect's motive and opportunity. In order to identify a potential suspect, an agent will question associates, family and witnesses for unusual incidents which may indicate either motive or opportunity.

Once a suspect is identified, agents will:

- Pull and examine any surveillance data from the scene of the crime and the surrounding area.
- Question the suspect's associates to determine the suspect's knowledge of the victim.
- Question the suspect regarding his relationship with the victim and determine if the suspect has an alibi for the determined time of death as determined by coroner or pathologist.
- Conduct surveillance, undercover operations and deeper investigations of a suspect including corroborating suspect's alibi.

The traditional interview of an arrested suspect accompanied by legal representation still takes place. While cortex hacking a suspect would theoretically prove a suspect's guilt or innocence, it is also a direct violation of the 5th Democratic Principle if applied without consent.

Standard Issue Equipment

All NSO agents are provided with a small clothing budget to cover the cost of work-appropriate attire. This budget does not allow for clothing that is particularly stylish or fashionable so agents will often use personal funds to upgrade their wardrobes.

Along with a Link phone, nanocomp with identification information and a badge, all agents are supplied a standard issue 10mm Traylor Police Special and a non-rigid armoured vest. Other equipment may be temporarily issued, depending on investigation requirements. This includes:

- Surveillance equipment including detectors, binoculars, image intensifiers, scopes, bugs, taps, microphones and makeup kits.
- Scientific and lighting equipment including imagers, analysers, imaging dust, isolation tents with cleanlocks, sampling kits, lamps and chemlights.
- Communicators and portacomps with appropriate crackers, translators, guides and other law enforcement software.
- Restraints and vehicle disabling equipment.
- Non-lethal weapons including sonic stunners and neural disruptors.
- Traylor Model 10 riot guns.
- Unmarked sedans and sport utility vehicles.
- Surveillance drones including flying disk camera platforms and Aquitaine D-5 remote piloted drones.
- Identifying gear such as NSO-labelled caps, cloaks and dry climate survival garb.

All field offices come equipped with a small armoury that is stocked to equip the in-house emergency response team. The Ellis field office, representative of field offices across human space, has been assigned the following paramilitary gear:

- Stracher MP-67 submachineguns.
- Full-body inertial armour.
- Helmets with internal displays and limited atmospheric filters.
- Smoke, gas, flash-bang and stun grenades.
- Breaching tools including battering rams and explosives.
- Stracher Faustus CD gas/baton launchers.
- Rockwell 12-81 Magnum sniper rifles.
- Thermal-visual camouflage sets.
- Bulldog battlesuits (TL11).

Agents with cybernetic enhancements or replacements are rare unless the agent has military experience. These cybernetics are typically limited to audio and visual enhancements for SWAT specialists.

Profit Without Honour

WARNING: IN ORDER TO PRESERVE SUSPENSE, PLAYERS SHOULD READ NO FURTHER. REFEREE'S MATERIAL FOLLOWS.

The Product

Psychiatric treatments have eliminated most chemical dependencies in the developed world. Outside of Core world nations with strong theocratic ties, most governments have also decriminalised many previously controlled substances, such as cannabis, opioids and other plant extracts.

However, not everyone in the Core reaps the benefits of liberal narcotics policies. Urban blight zones, such as Libreville's Mudville slums or the megacity ghettos of the Inca Republic, are home to the marginalised and neglected. It is from these areas, along with hidden labs in higher tier nations, that high-tech and harmful recreational drugs are manufactured. One of the most dangerous is the classification of drug known as neuroscriptors.

Neuroscriptors were developed in parallel to human DNA modification procedures in the mid-2250s. While the human body's ability to survive in extreme climates was adjusted, neurochemists worked on amplifying cognitive abilities through tailored viruses and proteins. Initial results were promising but testing ceased after the Gene Riots. The test data was leaked to ProVolution sympathisers and development continued in black labs.

By the late 2280s, the first waves of neuroscriptor abuse hit major metropolitan areas. Effects varied by the specific chemical makeup of the dose but users dubbed the new narcotic *Scribble* after its effects on neural pathways. Ingested via capsule, inhalant or patch, users catalogued the different effects of Scribble with a system of colour codes. Dealers adapted this system to sell their wares. *Pinks* induce an impenetrable feeling of sexual euphoria, *Yellows* create intense curiosity or fascination, *Greys* slow the perception of time, *Reds* cause violent and sociopathic feelings, and *Blues* suppress all emotions. Combined Scribble formulas, often called *remixes* or *stripes*, attempt to combine the effects though the result is a less intense high. For example, Pink-Yellow cocktails are popular party drugs.

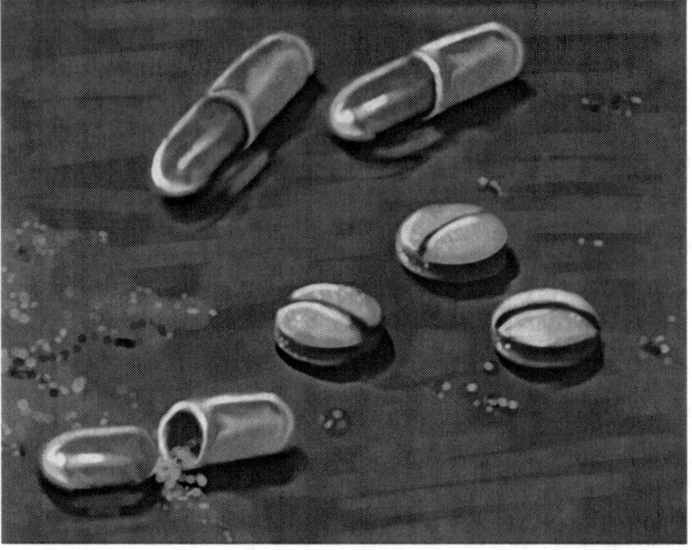

The dangers of Scribble are well documented. Psychological dependency is common as are aphasia, seizures, depression, paranoia and other neurological illnesses. The risks of Scribble use are so great that the American federal government has banned its production and distribution. Governments dosing soldiers or unsuspecting populations with Scribble is a common trope in electronic entertainment but even the most aggressive military programs find little use for brain-damaged troops.

Scribble reached Ellis in 2295. Colonial economic opportunities prevented the formation of a traditional criminal class to support its distribution. But the rural population of the colony presented unforeseen issues. An extremely low population density combined with a lack of immediate access to modern therapies has resulted in a greater percentage of substance abuse than its Core or urban colonial counterparts. In Liberty County, legal and illegal narcotic abuse is the third leading cause of death after environmental exposure and vehicle or farm equipment accidents.

Law enforcement has one advantage in its fight against rising distribution. Scribble requires hospital-level sterility and expensive lab equipment to manufacture. Attempts at 'backyard' manufacturing have all resulted in failure as exposed protein and virus cultures die almost immediately.

Use of Scribble temporarily grants the Annoying and Sensory Impaired Disadvantages for 2D hours. The use of Red also grants the Manic Disadvantage. After the effects of a dose, a character must make a Very Difficult (-4) Endurance check to avoid taking the Sickly disadvantage for 1D days. See *2300AD*, pg. 105, for more details on Disadvantages.

The Zagerman Organisation

At the start of the adventure, the player characters and the NSO are aware that a major Scribble distribution group exists is on the rise. The Liberty County Sheriff's Department is tracking the activities of a crew of local dealers but for every arrest made a replacement dealer appears. Surveillance has revealed a kingpin's name, Si Zagerman, but records for this individual do not exist in any criminal or licensing system on the planet.

Si Zagerman was born in 2267 to a family of struggling but independent minded homesteaders in Liberty. His father was almost a victim of a violent land grab scheme and, in the 2270s, was arrested several times on false charges. As a result, the elder Zagerman was extremely suspicious of government overreach and taught his son to 'stay off the radar.' A teenage Si Zagerman moved into the Liberty domes in 2282 and brought his friends Edwin LaPlante, a one-time vehicle thief, and Sonja Kraus, the daughter of a German xenophobe and survivalist, with him.

Zagerman's crew began working as freelance smugglers. Beginning in 2283 they eliminated rival groups to win mafia don Nicky Bruno's AmeriCo drug packages. By 2296, the group had control of the profitable Ft. Patton-City-Spaceport triangle and were the leading Scribble dealers.

The organisation has bolstered its ranks by absorbing other crews and hiring new employees. Zagerman is the group's de facto leader. LaPlante handles the organisation's day-to-day operations as well as outside negotiations and Kraus is in charge of security, contract killings and intimidation. Both Zagerman and LaPlante have isolated themselves from the actual drug operations and only concern themselves with money laundering. Zagerman keeps criminal defence attorney Erin Cross on retainer as an advisor and legal representative. Cross holds a leadership seat with the Ellis Bar Association and uses her influence to intimidate government lawyers.

Below the group's leadership are the actual dealers. A crew's lead dealer receives a percentage of the profit made on a batch of drugs which is used to pay underlings. There are three groups of dealers, each assigned to one point in the F-C-S triangle. Dealer crews are primarily made up of minors which makes prosecution efforts difficult. Judges are hesitant to turn an impressionable minor over to the Bureau of Criminal Rehabilitation. Crew leaders tend to be older and more experienced dealers who have been promoted by Edwin LaPlante.

The Spaceport Crew is made up of Beata Rodriguez (crew leader and age 23), Greg Chin (age 17), Corie Janowski (age 22), Harold Nnoruom (age 16), Ryan Corbett (age 19) and Tomas Ortiz (age 17).

The Ft. Patton Crew is made up of Thom Hammond (crew leader and age 25), Abdullah El-Sayed (age 20), Olawale Iwu (age 17), Devera Jackson (age 16), Ajayi Obi (age 18) and Allie McClintock (age 18).

The City Crew is made up of Terrance Schroeder (crew leader and age 25), Dale Meyer (age 19), Victoria O'Connell (age 16), Colby Brown (age 16), Jun Li (age 17) and Kaitlin Wolf (age 18).

Sonja Kraus operates as the head of security, handling drug deliveries from the manufacturing plant personally. She is also a 'cleaner,' removing possible evidence against the organisation and eliminating witnesses who cannot be bribed. As the organisation operates with a zero-tolerance policy regarding cooperating with law enforcement, she kills crew members who are in danger of becoming police informants. She typically keeps five-to-six other soldiers on immediate call at all times.

The organisation maintains a few legitimate business fronts through which money is laundered. The organisation owns a vehicle repair service near the Liberty Spaceport, as well as a brothel, which the Zagermans use as a headquarters, a Nigerian bar and grill and a ground survey supply shop in the city proper. State auditor Cruz Friedman is a silent partner in all of the organisation's legitimate operations and quietly handles government-level bribes, including paying off sheriff's deputies, on Zagerman's behalf.

Miyuki Gould, an AmeriCo junior Vice-President of Sales, oversees the manufacturing of Scribble in AmeriCo secret labs. These labs are hidden in AmeriCo facilities. The largest operation is located in the convenience food packaging plant near the Liberty domes. Gould's superiors are aware of activities and expect regular kickbacks from her.

Zagerman is hot-tempered and prone to violence against perceived threats but is also very shrewd. LaPlante is more of a businessman and intellect. He is determined to shift the organisation's income to less risky and legal sources. Kraus has a fearsome reputation in the underworld but is friendly and very good-natured with her friends and even most 'civilians' – individuals not associated with a criminal enterprise or law enforcement.

The Cast of Profit Without Honour

- Avery, William – Proprietor of The Gun Shop.
- Bailey, Douglas – Murdered witness to the Ronald Terrell murder.
- Brodie, Stuart – Friend of Ronald Terrell and member of the Sons of Liberty.
- Chin, Greg – Teenage drug dealer. Reports to Beata Rodriguez.
- Corbett, Ryan – Teenage drug dealer. Reports to Beta Rodriguez.
- Cross, Erin – Powerful local attorney representing the Zagerman organisation. Member of the Ellis Bar Association.
- De Lisi, Fosco – Zagerman Organisation soldier who reports to Sonja Kraus.
- Elias, Staff Sgt. Robert – US Army black marketeer.
- Friedman, Cruz – Ellis state auditor and backroom business partner with the Zagerman organisation.
- Gould, Miyuki – AmeriCo manager and Scribble manufacturer.
- Hammond, Thom – Zagerman organisation lieutenant/ crew chief.
- Janowski, Corie – Beata Rodriguez's crew lieutenant.
- Kapinos, Karli – NSO Supervising Special Agent and the player characters' direct supervisor.
- Kramer, Wolf – Cruz Friedman's personal driver and gofer.
- Kraus, Sonja – Si Zagerman's lead enforcer.
- LaPlante, Edwin – Si Zagerman's partner and day-to-day business manager.
- MacDonald, Todd – Repair technician at the Desert Dollhouse brothel.
- Nnoruom, Harold – Teenage drug dealer. Reports to Beata Rodriguez.
- Ortiz, Tomas – Teenage drug dealer. Reports to Beta Rodriguez.
- Pedersen, Major Lars – US Army liaison to the Ellis NSO field office.
- Park, Xander – Assistant US Attorney and lead prosecutor on the Zagerman investigation.
- Raman, Arjun – Private security officer and witness to the Ronald Terrell murder.
- Rodriguez, Beata – Zagerman organisation lieutenant/ crew chief who was recently acquitted of a murder charge.
- Terrell, Ronald – Murdered member of the Sons of Liberty gang.
- Zagerman, Si – Mysterious head of the Zagerman organisation.

Corporate Extraterritoriality

In 2300, certain transnational corporations are granted extraterritorial permission from host nation governments. From a law enforcement perspective, this means that TransNat property is sovereign territory and is treated like a diplomatic embassy. AmeriCo is free to do what it wishes on its property, including manufacturing illegal narcotics. If a government wishes to redress a grievance with a corporate entity, it must do so through proper channels. In the case of America, that would be the US State Department's diplomatic service. See *Libreville: Core of Corruption* for background and history information on TransNats.

The Briefing

At the beginning of the adventure, the player characters are sworn agents of the National Security Office. Special Agents hold twice weekly briefings at the Liberty field office with their Supervising Special Agent, Karli Kapinos. Kapinos monitors her agents' caseloads and assigns new cases as they open.

American government offices are no longer dreary, cubicle-filled affairs. Traditional office support roles have been replaced by simple AIs and low-security work, such as public relations, can be handled by remote employees. To encourage collaboration, teams of Special Agents work in face-to-face groups in comfortable but conservatively decorated spaces. Work stations are set to an agent's preference, ranging from flat panel displays to VR interfaces with haptic response devices. Conference rooms with holotanks, projectors and interactive walls and a comfortable kitchen and lounge area are also available. Located below the main floor is the field office's armoury, motor pool and secured IT hardware.

As the briefing begins, the SSA and the player characters are joined in their conference room by Assistant US Attorney Xander Park. Park is of Korean descent and is a recent Justice Department appointee from Earth. He is affable with a rather raunchy sense of humour, so most Special Agents enjoy his company, but he is also a consummate professional. Park is the field office's liaison to the federal court system and lead prosecutor on most cases the NSO charges.

Kapinos begins with an announcement.

'Your current cases are being reassigned to other agents,' she says. 'SAC Jiménez has formally approved a Liberty County Sheriff's Department investigation transfer request to the NSO.'

Kapinos begins her summary of the case. Referees are free to read the dialog as presented or improvise and allow player characters to ask questions.

'Your target is the Zagerman Organisation, a small drug trafficking outfit based in Liberty County. The LCSD have

positively identified a handful of low-level dealers operating across the area. Local narcotics units have engaged in undercover drug buys and arrested individuals on intent to sell controlled substances. However, this has had little-to-no effect on drug traffic. Also, as those arrested have been minors, prosecutors are hesitant to hand them over to the Bureau of Criminal Rehabilitation on Earth. Drug dealers in the Core are usually adults so this is a legal murky area and uniquely colonial issue that's tied up in juvenile courts on Earth.'

Kapinos runs her hand on a touch surface on the conference room table. A holographic mug shot appears over the table, that of a young Hispanic woman.

'This is Beata Rodriguez, age 23. She's a lieutenant with the Zagerman crew. She was accused of killing a Sons of Liberty gang member, one Ronald Terell, in Eagle's Nest.'

The player characters know that the town of Eagle's Nest consists of short term housing and entertainment facilities for spacers and residences for Liberty Spaceport workers. The player characters also know that the Sons of Liberty gang is a growing problem on Ellis but is still held in check by local police. Kapinos continues.

'There were two eye witnesses, Arjun Raman, an off-duty private security officer, and Douglas Bailey, a maintenance technician. Raman actually saw the shooting and Bailey heard it. Raman gave a voluntary and clean session in a Cortescan, which backed up his original statement, but he recanted it while on the courtroom stand. Bailey gave an honest testimony but he was killed five days ago. His body was found near the site of Terell's remains. We believe the Zagermans threatened or bribed the witnesses but when Bailey refused he was executed as a warning to others.'

Kapinos waves her hand over the table sensors and the hologram morphs into a frozen drone surveillance image. A clean-cut Caucasian man with a close-trimmed van dyke and casual sport jacket stares back at the camera.

'This is Edwin LaPlante, age 34. He had some run-ins with law enforcement as a youth. His parents paid restitution on his behalf for personal vehicles he stole. Including a state-owned hover jeep. He has no criminal record after age 18 when he moved to the Liberty domes. He was at the Rodriguez trial seven days ago with this individual.'

Another wave of her hand and a mug shot of a hard-faced Caucasian woman with dark hair tied in intricate braids appears.

'Sonja Kraus, also age 34. A possible childhood friend. She's the daughter of a German immigrant; an old-fashioned, gun-toting survivalist. She's linked in several gangland murders but prosecutors have been unable to gather enough evidence for a charge to stick. It's believed she works with the Zagermans as an enforcer or assassin. Most likely Kraus and LaPlante attended the trial in order to intimidate the witness.'

The hologram projector clicks off.

'The Zagermans control the profitable drug territory known as the F-C-S Triangle; Fort Patton, the Liberty domes and the spaceport. Unfortunately, the ostensible head of the Zagermans, Si Zagerman, is a complete unknown. He has no vehicle licenses on record, he doesn't utilises banks and he never shows his face in public.'

'SAC Jiménez has promised to assist AUSA Park in delivering the organisation's leadership. If we remove the heads, the drug trade will die down. Mr. Park will be happy to answer your questions.'

Park looks at the player characters, expectant.

Possible Questions and Answers

How could Zagerman not be listed in any databases?

'This isn't the Core. It's easy to stay off the grid on a colony world. Your average criminal has been arrested at least once and has a record in a government database. Zagerman was never arrested as an adult and if he was arrested as a minor the record was expunged at age 18. Also, while Ellis is a colony world, it's legally a state of the Union. The American Extrasolar Colonial Administration keeps records of all colonists on Hermes and King but on this planet it's the jurisdiction of the state government. If he never filed personal taxes, never had an employer who filed on his behalf and never filed for government assistance, he would be an unknown entity. Also, even if we could convince the Ellis government to cooperate, biometric scanners and cameras are easy to fool so we don't risk cluttering them with bad data on law abiding citizens.

'Then again, he may have a record and we aren't looking in the right place.'

What else do you know about Kraus or LaPlante?

'Edwin LaPlante was born on 9 September '66. Two parents, both living. Farmers in Fairview. Detailed criminal record was expunged by the state in '84.

'Sonja Kraus was born on 14 July '66. Immigration record on father, Johann Kraus, formerly of the Rhine Metroplex, Germany. Father has a short arrest record which consists of a handful of public intoxication arrests and an arrest for an aggravated assault against a neighbour in Fairview. Current location, unknown. Sonja Kraus was arrested for the transport of Lv20,000 worth of Scribble in '98. Her lawyer, one Erin Cross, talked the judge down to a fine and probation. The Liberty County Sheriff's Department has flagged her as a Person of Interest in two unsolved murders. Local surveillance often places her with LaPlante.'

Why weren't the witnesses provided protection by the county sheriffs?

'The fact that this case is now in the hands of the NSO should be your first clue. Neither the LCSD nor the Ellis State Police have the manpower, training or resources to handle serial homicides or organised crime cases. They deal with theft complaints and rescue stranded travellers. Until the locals decide that a good local constabulary is worth a tax increase, there may be more witness deaths.'

You said that Arjun Raman provided a Cortescan record. What was the result?

'The technicians were able to pull a six second record. According to it, Mr. Raman was turning a corner into a dimly lit alley. As his vision adjusted to the shift in illumination, he saw muzzle flashes from Ms. Rodriguez's weapon silhouetted by a male figure who appeared to be falling. Mr. Raman ducked back around the corner to take cover. When Rodriguez was gone he found the body of Mr. Terrell.

'According to the techs, Raman's "fight-or-flight" adrenaline surge during the shooting prevented any further memory readings.'

What physical evidence did the LCSD recover from each crime scene?

'The locals don't have good quality forensic kits so their blood spatter analysis was inconclusive, other than it matched the victims. The state's case rested primarily on the medical examiner's report, the Cortescan results and witness testimony. Bailey had nothing out of the ordinary on his person. Terrell was carrying an unfired Chinese knockoff variant on the C4 Wallet Gun.'

What did the medical examiner's report say about the remains of Terrell or Bailey?

'Terrell had four entry wounds on his upper and centre dorsal region. The angle of the shots fired indicates that Terrell may have been knocked to his knees either before Rodriguez opened fire or the first shot knocked him down. Rodriguez's lawyer successfully argued that her client, an unaugmented woman who is barely 1.5 m, does not have the strength to knock down a 102 kg male. It helped cast a shadow of a doubt on the prosecution's case.

'Bailey had a single wound located at the left temporal lobe of the skull. Single blunt force trauma indicating impact with a small pipe or even a rock. It broke the skull and shoved bone fragments into the brain tissue. The victim haemorrhaged to death.'

What equipment is available for this investigation?

'Standard crime scene investigation or surveillance equipment and drones are available to you. If you want to engage in communications surveillance, you will need to provide enough evidence for an affidavit that proves 'exhaustion' – that you can't continue your investigation any other way.'

Where should we start?

'I would suggest looking over the homicide scenes in Eagle's Nest. I wouldn't trust the accuracy of the LCSD crime scene investigators. You could find and interview witnesses, identify any legitimate business connections the Zagermans may have, find and stake out Scribble dealing locations in order to ID members of crews, follow up with the Sons of Liberty, and start hunting for an ID on Si Zagerman.'

The Investigation

Profit Without Honour is not a linear adventure. Players may begin anywhere they choose and follow leads to their logical conclusion (or not). However, many players may feel overwhelmed, unsure of where to look or – if they misinterpret a piece of evidence – frustrated when a trail turns cold. Referees are encouraged to roleplay SSA Kapinos as an intelligent advisor. Kapinos is an experienced senior agent and is likely to have ideas player characters did not consider. The referee should never direct players to a piece of evidence but rather suggest courses of action that will lead a player to a piece of evidence.

The key to player success in the adventure is ensuring that the player characters are able to either directly or remotely observe Si Zagerman engaged in a criminal act. In order to do that, they will need to work their way up the chain of the Zagerman organisation. This may mean identifying and observing dealers, turning NPCs into confidential informants and following money trails. The Zagerman organisation is not stupid – it is made up of professional criminals who, while not necessarily the most loyal individuals, are both business savvy enough to keep doing what they are doing and live in fear of Sonja Kraus.

Investigate Skill Tests

Profit Without Honour focuses on a criminal investigation. As calling for an Investigate test each step of the way would make for a boring adventure, gathering evidence requires several additional skills including Recon, Persuade and Streetwise.

It is possible that player characters will fail needed skill tests in order to gather a much needed piece of the puzzle. In this instance, the referee reserves the right to call for a Difficult (-2), Investigate, Int or Edu skill test in order to gather a clue that player characters might otherwise miss. This skill test should only be used if all other options have been exhausted.

As the referee will play the part of AUSA Park, he will be responsible for determining if the player characters have done their job. A good rule of thumb is, if the player characters have exhausted most, if not all, of their leads, Park will allow them to utilise electronic surveillance.

What's Really Going On: Beata Rodriguez

Under orders from Si Zagerman, Beata Rodriguez executed Ronald Terrell, a low ranking member of the Sons of Liberty, for attempting to sell drugs in Zagerman territory. Rodriguez approached Terrell as a potential buyer but when Terrell turned around and bent down to retrieve a hidden stash of Scribble, she shot him with her Traylor Arms M-20. Rodriguez acted rashly in killing Terrell near Eagle's Nest's heavily travelled Sega Strip. The shots attracted witnesses and Rodriguez was unaware of this. Without Rodriguez's knowledge, Sonja Kraus intimidated the two witnesses to the shooting. When Douglas Bailey refused to keep quiet, he was shot in the cranium with an AS-3 sonic stunner by one of Kraus's soldiers, Fosco De Lisi. While technically a non-lethal weapon, a stunner contact can unleash enough blunt sonic force energy to shatter a quarter-sised piece of bone and cause massive haemorrhaging (see Researching an Unusual Murder on pg. 34).

What Zagerman and the other leaders do not know is that the execution of Bailey has left Rodriguez emotionally scarred and depressed. While she had no problem killing a fellow criminal in the name of 'business,' murdering two innocents was never her intention. The organisation's cold disregard for life has her shaken. A smart Special Agent may take advantage of this.

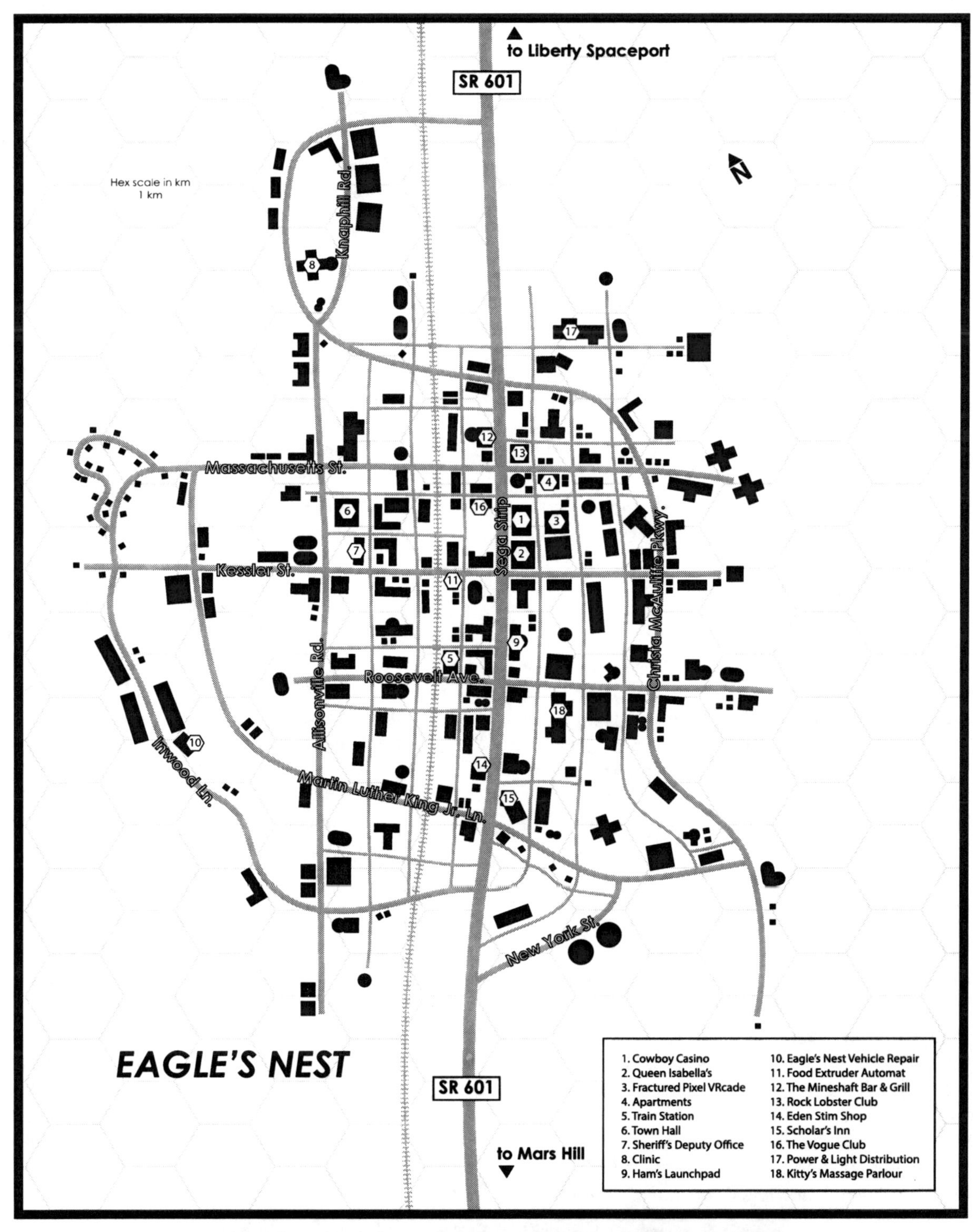

Scene of the Crime: The Sega Strip

The town of Eagle's Nest is located 15 km southeast of the Liberty Spaceport. Eagle's Nest serves a dual purpose as a location for spacers to engage in vice-related activities and as Liberty County's adult entertainment destination. It is a single 6 km section of Ellis SR 601 that is lined with chintzy hotels, taverns, greasy-spoon restaurants, low-stakes casinos, exotic dance revues, gift shops, stimshops, nerve parlours/brothels and virtual reality arcades. A series of wind break walls minimise the impact of wind and sandstorms on the facilities. Smaller service roads run parallel and perpendicular to the Strip and are the location of low-cost residences for spaceport employees and their dependents as well as nightlife addicts. Locals-only bars are situated off the main roads and tourists who stumble into the wrong establishment risk a brawl. Small family-owned businesses are sprinkled throughout the town.

During daylight hours, the Sega Strip is a depressing collection of one and two-story reinforced spraycrete buildings with solar collectors and electrostatic dust repellers mounted to the roofs. At night the street is lined with sparkling holograms, spray-on LEDs and even antique neon signs. Like most Liberty architecture, the majority of the buildings' mass is buried or located below ground.

Pedestrians are a mix of off-duty military personnel from Fort Patton, local farmers and ranchers on vacation, Canadian and Nigerian tourists, shuttle pilots from the Boise spaceport and interstellar merchant crews on shore leave.

Near the centre of the town is an airfilm train line station along with the town council office and the local Liberty County Sheriff's Department sub-station. Deputies use a light touch any typically intercede only in the case of violence.

Ronald Terrell was killed in the northeast-southwest alleyway between the Cowboy Casino and Queen Isabella's Love Ranch. Douglas Bailey was killed 60 metres to the north, at a service entrance just behind the Fractured Pixel VRcade. Desert climates are excellent at preserving evidence so long as it is blocked from the wind and dust. The player characters have access to the LCSD's crime scene images for comparison. Analysing the crime scenes will require an Average (+0) Investigate, Int, 1 hour check for each.

With a successful check on the Terrell murder scene, the following is revealed:

- Scuff marks on the ground and dried blood stains on the alley-side exterior wall of the Cowboy Casino, corroborated with distance from the wall, indicates the victim fell forward into a foetal position after impact from behind. Most likely the victim was shot while unaware.
- Witness testimony reported between three and four shots fired but no shell casings were retrieved by the LCSD. The player characters discover four 11x38mm casings on the roof of Queen Isabella's, 4.5 metres above and behind the alleged shooter's position. They were caught between an HVAC unit filter and electrostatic repeller bracket. The size of the shells and the ejection height indicates a very high-power sidearm, not one common in civilian or even law enforcement use. The firearm is most likely military issue and a quick check reveals an 80% probability of the firearm being a Traylor Arms M-20. If the player characters follow up on the firearm's history, go to Tracing Rodriguez's Firearm on pg. 33.
- On an Effect of 6+, the player characters discover two package of mixed Scribble pills wedged behind a tightly fitted but broken piece of spraycrete in the Cowboy Casino outer wall. One package is still sealed in airtight plastic and one open and half empty. Together they are worth nearly Lv1,500 indicating that the murder was not part of a robbery but rather a straight execution. The Zagerman organisation has enough product on hand that even Lv1,500 worth of drugs is not worth the time to steal.

With a successful check on the Bailey murder scene, the following is revealed:

- The blood spattering where Bailey fell does not match the patterning of a physical strike to the head. The blood patterns are uniform drips and pools from where the victim bled out on the spot but there is no indication of spray collecting on and being flung off a swinging object.
- The victim fell close to the rear exterior wall of the VRcade. But according to the position of the body and with the wounded side of the head facing the wall, the wall would prevent the perpetrator from enough swinging hard enough to shatter a skull. Therefore the wound must have been delivered through a mechanical or electronic device.
- On an Effect of 6+, the player characters discover that a 36-hour tractor repair garage around the corner is close enough to the scene to have possibly overheard anything on the night of the murder. One of the mechanics who was on duty during the night in question recalls hearing a brief, extremely high-pitched squeal which made him grit his teeth. The mechanic assumed a passing airfilm train had blown a compressor. See What's Really Going On: Beta Rodriguez on pg. 29 to see what the mechanic actually heard. If the player characters follow up on it, go to Researching an Unusual Murder on pg. 34.

Canvasing for Witnesses

Fearing for his life, Arjun Raman has left the Liberty area for a Nigerian enclave. If the player characters visit his residence, they will find it empty. According to neighbours, he has left no forwarding address and there is no one to track him.

If the player characters choose to canvas the Sega Strip crime scene area for witnesses, they should make an Average (+0) Recon, Int check. On a success they will notice that, on first glance what seems to be a commercial warehouse at the end of the alley is in fact a small apartment complex. One of the second floor apartments has a bedroom window overlooking the alley.

The current tenant is a woman named Kay Ballard. A retired and childless widow, Ballard sold her family farm three years ago and moved into the apartment to enjoy easy access to necessities and the freewheeling hustle and bustle of the Sega Strip. She now regrets her decision. The gang and drug activity are beginning to terrify the 75 year-old woman. Nervous to leave her home, she is also aware of the reach of the Zagerman Organisation and does not believe the police can help her.

If the player characters succeed on an Average (+0) Persuade, Soc, 10 minute check, Ballard will share what she knows. She was at home the night of Bailey's murder and was sitting in the dark, staring aimlessly out the window and listening to her late husband's rock-hop music collection. She had seen Bailey before. He often frequented the Fractured Pixel VRcade after work. She tells the player characters that Bailey walked out of the VRcade's rear door and walked past an open alley where another man quickly approached him from behind. The new man raised what appeared to be a small pistol or sonic stunner and pressed it to the back of Bailey's head. A loud squeal sounded and Bailey fell to the ground. The man quickly hurried away. Realising what had happened, Ballard quickly closed the sand storm shutters on her windows and stayed quiet.

Ballard describes the assailant as a tall and thin male, Caucasian with dark slicked back hair. He appeared to be in his late thirties or early forties and was wearing stylish rust-coloured desert survival clothing. Ballard is willing to testify and undergo a Cortescan session. Whoever killed Bailey appears to be an assassin, not a dealer.

The Sons of Liberty

Finding a local gathering place for members of the Sons of Liberty gang is as simple as a call on the LCSD sub-station in Eagle's Nest. The sub-station consists of a drunk tank, three marked cars and eight local sheriff's deputies more used to dealing with spacers on a bender than any sort of murder investigation. The deputies will be impressed with the player characters' federal credentials and offer any assistance they can. The deputies point the player characters to The Mousetrap, a local's-only drinking hole just north of Eagle's Nest.

From the highway, The Mousetrap appears to be a collection of a half dozen civilian vehicles parked next to a small hill built in the regolith. Upon closer inspection, they will notice the hill has a short set of stairs leading into it and a sliding airlock door. The airlock door is actually a commonly used dustlock system that pulls powdery fines from hair and clothing.

Inside, The Mousetrap is a small subterranean dome. A slowly twisting prism in the oculus above bathes the room in twisting rainbows. A circular bar sits in the centre, casks of local wine and off-world spirits and beers are guarded by a ruddy-faced bartender. Leaning against the bar and seated in the handful of tables which spiral outward, the patrons make up of two distinct archetypes – weather-beaten loners, mostly miners and farmers, and tough teenage males.

The Sons of Liberty are easily identifiable by their personalised desert survival clothing. Their tan keffiyehs, ball caps and jackets sport stylised American flag, Uncle Sam, eagle and coiled rattlesnake motifs. The gang members are hostile to law enforcement and if the player characters identify themselves as such or enter flashing their badges, the Sons will refuse to speak to the player characters without a successful Very Difficult (-4) Persuade, Soc or Int check. Use the Petty Thug 2 NPC, pg. 84 of the *Traveller Core Rulebook*, for the Sons.

Alternately, the player characters can approach the Sons in a friendlier, less aggressive style. If the player characters try to appeal to the Sons' sense of loyalty to their fallen comrade, Ronald Terrell, an Average (+0) Carouse or Diplomacy, Soc check will get one of the members talking, though hesitantly.

At age 15, Stuart Brodie is one of the younger members of the gang. When he joined the Sons, the older Terrell took a liking to him. Terrell acted as an informal mentor figure by showing Brodie the ropes of selling Scribble. The two became friends, sharing a fondness for baseball, local farm girls and *Bug Hunt*, a fictionalised interactive VR account of Foreign Legionnaires fighting Kaefers on Aurore. He was asleep at home when Terrell was killed and was traumatised by his murder. Though

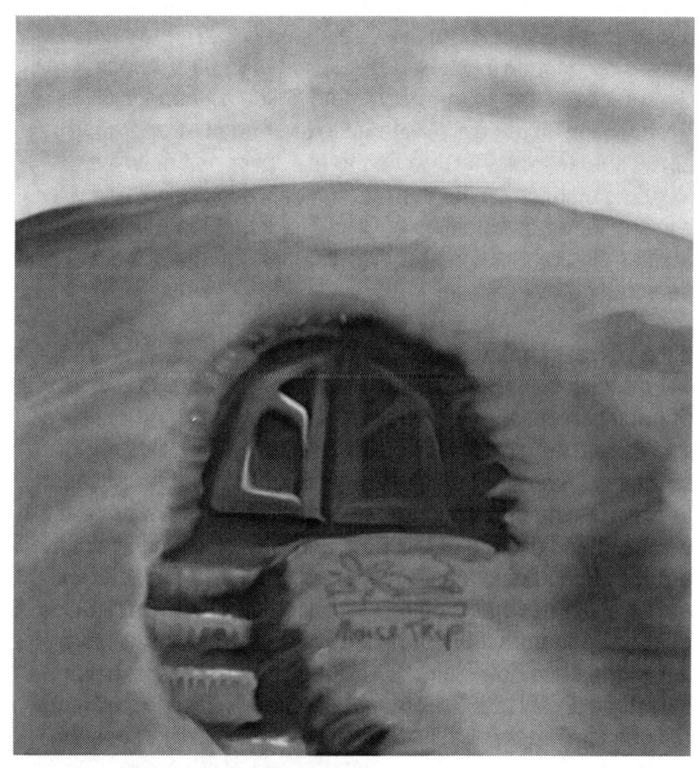

Brodie does not know the real names of the Zagerman Scribble dealers and soldiers in the spaceport area, he knows where they operate and can identify them by sight. Brodie is a good candidate for an informant if the player characters want to use him in their operations.

The current hotspots for the Zagerman dealers are Ham's Launchpad, a dance club on the Sega Strip, the airfilm train station at the spaceport and the Food Extruder food bar in Franklin, south of Eagle's Nest. See Staking Out the Dealers on pg. 32 for more information.

Business Connections

Edwin LaPlante runs the Zagerman Organisation's business arm which includes managing and overseeing fronts. If the player characters run a successful record search they will find that LaPlante's name is listed on licenses for the following businesses:

- Wheelwright Repair & Reconditioning, an automotive garage in Eagle's Nest.
- Skookum Jim's Survey Equipment, a ground survey supply shop in Liberty.
- Beautiful Shades Nigerian Restaurant, a bar and grill in Liberty.
- The Desert Dollhouse, a brothel in Liberty specialising in companion robots.

A successful Easy (+4) Streetwise, Int or Edu check will reveal that the Desert Dollhouse floor plan, with its easily secured rooms, would make for an ideal base of operations. If the player characters want to flip an employee into an informant, go to The Disgruntled Employee on pg. 35.

If the player characters are engaged in surveillance of the dealers (see Staking Out the Dealers on pg. 32), the referee should request an Easy (+4) Recon, Int, 48 hours, check. On a success, the player characters notice a Bridgeport Swift Raven luxury car pulling up to the Food Extruder food bar. A dealer hands a large bag to the driver and pulls away. Running a check on the vehicle's identification will reveal that it is registered to the office of Cruz Friedman, the Ellis state auditor. Behind the wheel is Wolf Kramer, Friedman's driver and personal gofer.

If the player characters pull the vehicle over and search it, they will discover a black neoprene bag filled with Lv50,000 worth of American dollar notes. Kramer has technically committed no crimes and the player characters cannot legally hold him. On a successful Average (+0) Persuade, Soc test, Kramer will admit to only running an errand for his employer. He is not privy to the wheeling and dealing of the state auditor's office, he is simply a driver. If the player characters seize the cash, the NSO will hold it until Friedman's office solicits for its return. The NSO is obligated to return it but the player characters will now have a link to the state government. This adventure does not cover an investigation of Cruz Friedman, but referees, if so inspired, may choose to have the NSO open a case against him. If not, the referee may have Kapinos explain that the NSO does not have the resources to pursue the lead at this time and investigations should focus on the original target.

Staking Out the Dealers

The ideal location for Scribble deals is one that sees a great deal of foot or vehicle traffic but is not under the watchful eye of law enforcement or civic-minded citizens. Beata Rodriguez's crew sticks to three primary locations, moving around to get the best coverage at peak foot and vehicle traffic times. Note that this adventure assumes the player characters will stake out locations near the murder site in Eagle's Nest in order to tie the case together. If the player characters look into the other two crews, the Ft. Patton Crew operates out of the city of Independence in western Liberty County, and the City Crew operates out of Liberty proper. Bars, clubs, warehouses, cheap restaurants, unguarded transport hubs and fuel stations all make for good dealer spots.

The first location is Ham's Launchpad, a popular club on Eagle's Nest's Sega Strip. The club opens at sunset when its holographic signage, a stylised chimpanzee in a 1950s spacesuit riding an ancient Saturn rocket, illuminates. The club features a large dance floor that shakes to countronica, fuzz-reggae and acid om pop music tracks. Pinks and Yellows are the popular drugs of choice and deals typically take place in darkened corners, of which there are many. Rodriguez's crew typically arrives around 16:00.

The second location is the Liberty Spaceport airfilm train station. The terminal sees a great deal of foot traffic, from incoming workers to outgoing visitors. Scribble dealers commonly station themselves outside of the terminal doors and only approach potential buyers who look like they might need a hit. All types of neuroscriptors are sold at the terminal, from Reds for off-planet merchant crews looking to start fights in local dive bars to Yellows or Blues for warehouse crews looking for distractions from their tedious jobs. Rodriguez's crew operates in the area from 07:30 until 10:00 and again at 13:00 until 15:00.

The third location is the Food Extruder in the town of Franklin, just south of Eagle's Nest. Franklin is primarily known for its retail and services industries that cater to local farm families. Agricultural machinery and equipment parts sold through Alberta Farmers' Collective-approved wholesalers and home décor from off-world vendors bring shoppers from kilometres around. While a Food Extruder is a common site in the Core, the chain of food bars is considered a rare novelty on Ellis and is a draw for locals. Scribble customers are typically in a family unit and range from depressed parents who purchase Blues to curious teenagers who find the experience of Yellow novel. Rodriguez's crew is in the Food Extruder during daylight and early evening hours when they are not operating elsewhere.

Each drug crew in the Zagerman organisation uses what's known as a stash house. A stash house is an easily secured but unused building or room that drug dealers use to store their product prior to a deal. The stash house may also hold serve as an informal armoury, holding the crew's illegal weapons. Scribble is delivered on a daily or as-needed basis to the stash house by Sonja Kraus or one of her soldiers. These deliveries are fresh from the AmeriCo packaging plant and are mixed in crates with sealed packages of convenience food. From there, smaller bags of the product are carried by dealers to their spots. Dealers will make regular runs back to refill their pockets. Dealers do not know where the drugs originate and most are fearful enough not to be curious.

The player characters may choose to stake out drug dealers but will need to know where to look beforehand. Local police are aware of deals taking place at the airfilm terminal. In order to find other locations, the player characters will need to find an informant, see The Sons of Liberty on pg. 31, or spend a great deal of time asking around while undercover. A Difficult (-2) Investigate, Int or Soc skill, 24 hours, check will uncover one location at the referee's discretion.

The Spaceport Crew, see Background: The Zagerman Organisation on pg. 25, is not aggressive in soliciting buyers. The most charismatic member of the crew, the 'boiler,' targets marks and talks potential buyers to the actual drug seller. The seller takes the buyer's money and signals a nearby runner, a junior member of the crew, to deliver the purchased drugs several metres away from the money exchange. The runner only carries enough drug doses to cover the purchase and returns to the 'stash' on a motor bike to refill for the next buyer. The stash, which contains the full drug package for the day, is the crew's livelihood and is guarded by the crew chief or his/her lieutenant. The guard is typically armed. In order to minimise the police from hitting crews with illegal weapons charges, no one other than stash guards are permitted to carry firearms.

A properly vetted informant, such as Stuart Brodie, see Sons of Liberty on pg. 31, can be used to not only point out when and where a crew is operating but can identify the various members of Beata Rodriguez's crew. If the player characters attempt to identify members of the crew on their own, they can attempt an Average (+0) Recon, Int, 2 hour check. The dealers are on the watch for police so player characters who are in Close or Personal Range will need to make a Routine (+2) Deception, Int check to avoid being spotted.

Player characters may select to use drones with remote sensors to quietly identify the dealers. A player character should serve as drone pilot and make a Difficult (-2) Remote Operations, Dex check to keep the drone hidden. If the dealers spot the drones, they will walk away. Either Beata Rodriguez or her lieutenant, Corie Janowski, will open fire on the drone until it is destroyed. Use the Dangerous Thug NPC, pg. 84 of the *Traveller Core Rulebook*, for Rodriguez and Janowski. Rodriguez carries a Traylor Arms M-20 and Janowski carries a Hancock 9-23 Enforcer.

If the player characters successfully identify the dealers, they will have names and descriptions for each one. They will also have locations of drug stashes, see Stash Raid on pg. 35. This will make it easier to identify which crew member is interacting with the Zagerman leadership.

Identifying Si Zagerman

Positively identifying Si Zagerman can be accomplished in a number of ways, including combining approaches.

- *Approach 1:* The most obvious method is to arrest one of Zagerman's lieutenants. Low-level street dealers have no contact with him (or, at least, do not know they have). A player character can attempt a formal interrogation but this will require an Extremely Difficult (-5) Persuade, Soc or Str, 8 hour, skill test. The lieutenants are selected for their loyalty and ability to hold up under duress, especially given if they cooperate with the police their lives are forfeit.
- *Approach 2:* The player characters can attempt to flip a Scribble user into a confidential informant (see Confidential Informants on pg. 22). At the referee's discretion, good roleplaying will lower the difficulty of or even eliminate the need for a skill check. On a success, a willing CI will have a description for the player characters in 1D+2 days.
- *Approach 3:* If the player characters included street level contacts in character generation or have been investigating other leads, they can make an Average (+0) Underworld, Int or Soc, 1D+1 days check.
- *Approach 4:* If the player characters make contact with Edwin LaPlante's parents, Vernon and Loretta, a successful Average (+0) Persuade, Soc will convince the couple to, reluctantly, share the most recent photograph of both Edwin and Si Zagerman in their possession. The image is dated 2281 which is when both men were 14. A Routine (+2) Computers, Edu or Int check using face enhancement software will create a useable likeness. A Marginal Failure will still pass though the player characters will need a more recent snapshot if they want to use any kind of recognition software.

Sonja Kraus's father, Johann, maintains no permanent residence and is nearly impossible to find.

On a success, the player characters have uncovered a reliable and recent image of Si Zagerman. Zagerman is 1.8 meters in height with a thin but very muscular build. He keeps his dark hair close-cropped and sports a thin moustache and goatee. His taste in clothes and outdoor wear is trendy for colonial garb.

Tracing Rodriguez's Firearm

Set by the Jarvis-Thompsen Act of 2176, an automatic firearm, like the M-20, is considered a Class III weapon. A Federal Weapons Permit is required to legally possess one. A Simple (+6) Admin, Edu check will confirm that Beata Rodriguez is not listed in the DoJ database as a permit holder.

Current military weapons often end up on the black market.

Greedy quartermasters may 'accidentally' lose a shipment or simply steal them from an armoury. If the player characters follow up with the military, a visit to Fort Patton is in order.

Fort Patton's NSO liaison is Major Lars Pedersen, a tall male of obvious Norwegian heritage. Pedersen greets the player characters at the fort's gate and escorts them to his office in the administrative centre. If the player characters explain the reason for their visit, Pedersen seems pained. He explains that Fort Patton is a tough billet, especially for soldiers who consider the Core to be their home. It is a thankless job that can lead to difficulties when a soldier rotates back. Many troops will take advantage of the local black markets in order to pad their bank accounts or to escape. Drugs abuse is on the rise, especially Scribble. The military police company does an admirable job in tackling contraband moving in and out of the base. However, goods slip through.

Pedersen offers to summon the base's armoury staff. If the player characters agree, the staff assembles in a nearby conference room. However, 30 minutes after the summoning, Pedersen notices that Staff Sgt. Robert Elias is not in attendance. Pedersen radios the gate and the sentries report that Elias passed through 5 minutes earlier.

Elias was tipped off to the player characters' visit by a corporal in the administration centre. He is now fleeing the base and heading for an unannounced meet with Thom Hammond and the Ft. Patton Crew (see The Zagerman Organisation on pg. 25). If he is not intercepted he will arrive in the city of Independence. While its population is comparable to Libety's, Independence is primarily a shipping hub for farmers in the western townships. It is home to several dozen square kilometres of temperature-controlled warehouses and grain silos filled with produce along with pens of meat animals waiting for transport. Thom Hammond has set up in Klondike Ike's Bar & Grill and uses a nearby, unused feed bin for a drug stash.

If the player characters do not pursue, Elias will arrive at Klondike Ike's in a panic, offering Thom Hammond a crate of fragmentation grenades in exchange for protection and a ticket off-world. Hammond will become angry with Elias when he realises Elias has possibly led law enforcement to him. He will have Elias dragged into the alley behind Klondike Ike's and shot. The crew will then set up their operation elsewhere in Independence.

If the player characters decide to give chase in their vehicle, Elias is driving an M1040, the standard American military light utility vehicle (use the Rangestar Range Truck, Militia Version, pg. 148, *Tools for Frontier Living*). Use the sample Guard NPC, pg. 277 of *2300AD*, for Elias. If the driving player character succeeds in an opposed Drive (wheeled), Dex check, the player characters will overtake Elias's vehicle.

If the player characters have immediate access to a high speed drone, the controlling character may make an opposed Remote Operations, Dex check vs. Elias's Drive (wheeled), Dex. If successful, the drone will spot Elias's vehicle. Via remote, the player characters will see Elias enter Klondike Ike's. Three minutes later, Elias will exit the rear of the bar into an alley with two men holding his arms. A third will press a handgun to his head and fire, leaving Elias laying face-down. Shortly thereafter, a group of four men and two women leave the bar and, using small personal vehicles, will scatter across Independence. The vehicles will be ditched a few blocks away and the dealers will disappear into various buildings and irrigation ducts to escape observation.

If the player characters manage to capture Elias before he reaches Klondike Ike's, a successful Difficult (-2) Persuade, Str or Soc check will get him talking. Elias will admit to exchanging an M-20 autopistol and quietly removing it from Fort Patton's records for a package of Scribble which he was selling on base. He confirms Beata Rodriguez as the recipient of the firearm. If the player characters have successfully gathered the physical evidence from the Sega Strip, it is enough to satisfactorily tie Rodriguez to the Terrell murder. If the player characters successfully submit an affidavit to AUSA Park, he will request an electronic tap on Rodriguez's communications (go to Taps & Bugs on pg. 36) as soon as the player characters acquire her Link ID.

If the player characters attempt to bust Hammond's crew, go to Stash Raid on pg. 35.

Researching an Unusual Murder

If the player characters do a data search on unsolved murders with victims resembling the late Douglas Bailey, they should make a Simple (+6) Admin or Informatics, Edu check. On a success, the player characters discover a record matching their search parameters.

The victim was a 19 year-old college student named Luisa Calderón who attended Ellis University. She was found dead in the bed of her first-floor campus dormitory room. The door had been locked and the window was left open. Plastic fragments indicated the window's mechanical lock had been quickly jimmied open from outside. Her friends recalled seeing Calderón in a discussion with a dark-haired woman named 'Bea' the afternoon before her death. The victim behaved as if she knew the woman but the description provided did not match any known relatives. The dorm's occupants reported hearing a high pitched squeal the night of the killing, like a sound system going through a feedback loop. The cheap window glass in Calderón's room was also reported as cracked by campus police but with no apparent cause.

If the player characters visit the former crime scene, they should make an Average (+0) Investigate Int, 2 hour, check. On a success the player characters will discover cigarette butts scattered near a bench in the decorative scrub grass just outside the dorm building. A lab test at the NSO field office will pull the lip prints on the butts. Most of the prints match students enrolled at Ellis University but five match a police biometric record for Fosco De Lisi, a suspected Zagerman soldier. De Lisi has been twice arrested but the police have been unable to make a charge stick. If the player characters want to go after De Lisi, go to Hunting for the Hitman on pg. 36.

What's Really Happening: Luisa Calderón met Si Zagerman at a local club three months ago. Calderón became Zagerman's girlfriend though her friends were unaware of the relationship. When she discovered that Zagerman kept other women on the side, she became jealous, threatening to spill his business to the police if he continued to see them. Zagerman dispatched Rodriguez to 'encourage' Calderón to mind her own business. However, Rodriguez is not a natural killer and could not bring herself to harm Calderón after providing a rebuffed warning. After Rodriguez reported back, Zagerman had Sonja Kraus dispatch one of her soldiers to take care of Calderón. While waiting for Calderón to settle into bed, Fosco De Lisi waited outside and smoked to pass the time. He then opened the window with a simple hand-made tool, climbed inside, killed her with a sonic stunner to the temple and exited back out the window to avoid detection.

The Disgruntled Employee

While the majority of the employees in the Desert Dollhouse are enhanced companion robots and are owned by the brothel, the brothel also employs a handful of service technicians. A tech named Todd MacDonald is the brothel's most efficient worker. He also harbours an unhealthy obsession for 'Misty,' one of the dolls he maintains.

Recently, Sonja Kraus and her soldiers held a party at the brothel. The party became violent and a thug broke Misty's limbs and shattered several internal components. MacDonald was heartbroken at the brutal treatment the Doll received.

The player characters have numerous options for determining if MacDonald will make for a suitable confidential informant. They may go undercover to the Desert Dollhouse. On a successful Average (+0) Recon, Int, 1 hour, check they will notice a sad-faced service tech leading a companion robot away to a service room. Alternately, the player characters may pull employee record files which include images. On a successful Easy (+4) Social Sciences (psychology) check, the player characters will perceive a heavy 'sadness' in MacDonald's eyes, an indicator that he would be sympathetic to law enforcement.

After the player characters approach MacDonald they will notice an intensely obsessive behaviour in him. His technician jumpsuit has food stains, he is slightly overweight and his hair and beard appear dishevelled. If Ellis was a Japanese colony, he would be considered an *otaku*. When discussing Misty, tears will stream down his face. He knows that the Zagermans use the brothel's VIP bar area for an office but he is forbidden from entering it without permission. The office is also behind a heavy and locked door with a guard standing just inside.

MacDonald is naturally craven but if the player characters succeed on a Very Difficult (-4) skill check (skills used are the referee's discretion) he will agree to spy for the NSO (see Taps and Bugs on pg. 36).

	Career Path	STR	DEX	END	INT	EDU	SOC
Todd MacDonald	Drifter (Scavenger) 3	4	6	4	10	10	2

Deception 2, Jack of All Trades 1, Mechanic 3, Recon 1
Traits: Coward, Fanatic/1, Dark Secret/1
DNAM: Dry World

Stash Raid

If the player characters decide to bust a drug stash they will need to acquire a warrant prior to a raid. During the raid itself, the crew leaders and crew lieutenants will attempt to hide or ditch their firearms in a refuse bin and the dealers will attempt to flee on foot. Player characters involved should make an opposed Athletics (Strength or Endurance), End check vs. the dealers to determine if a suspect is successfully restrained or if the suspect escapes. Use the Petty Thug 1 NPC, pg. 84 of the *Traveller Core Rulebook*, for dealers. The crews are smart enough not to shoot at police as violence, especially lethal violence, will make it impossible for a judge to grant bail.

Dealers do not carry identification but a biometric trace will identify each individual (see The Zagerman Organisation on pg. 25 for a list of members). Most, if not all, of the dealers will have a juvenile misdemeanour criminal record with charges of loitering or possession of illegal substances.

If the player characters attempt to recover Beata Rodriguez or Corie Janowski's firearms (or any other crew chiefs' weapons), they should make an opposed Investigate, Int check vs. the

crew leaderships' Deception, Int. Use the Dangerous Thug NPC, pg. 84 of the *Traveller Core Rulebook*, for Rodriguez and Janowski or any other crew leader. On a success the player characters successfully recover the hidden firearms.
If the player characters raid Rodriguez's crew, they will find the M-20 used in the Terrell murder. Unfortunately, the weapon is coated in a fingerprint resistant finish which makes directly tying it to Rodriguez impossible without corroborating evidence. Janowski's 9-23 is not registered to her but, under American law, as it is only a Class II weapon it is legal for her to possess it.

If the player characters examine the stash, they should make an Easy (+4) Investigate, Int check. At the referee's discretion, the following is discovered:

- Lv 2D x 1,000 worth of Scribble in mixed colours.
- 2D x 500 worth of promissory notes in American Dollars, stacked and bound in plastic bags.
- A small assortment of civilian revolvers, small-magazine semi-automatic pistols and hunting/home-defence shotguns, all unregistered.
- Opened and unopened AmeriCo-brand convenience foods including Flingadas™, Smackitos™ and Saffron Flavoured Beefixes™.
- A Link telephone number and the initials 'BR' recently scrawled on the back of a Lamb Crankizzers™ package. A successful Simple (+6) Computers, Int check will reveal that the number code is for a number for a prepaid, unregistered Link phone. Assuming the player characters raided Rodriguez's crew, the number will be for Rodriguez's 'business' Link.

  If the player characters order a handwriting analysis of the note, it will match Ryan Corbett's hand, assuming they can get a sample of his script. Corbett is a bit slow and needs to write numbers down in order to remember them.

  Important Note: This item will only be found at the Spaceport Crew stash house.

Hunting for the Hitman

Obtaining an arrest warrant for Fosco De Lisi will require at least two corroborating pieces of evidence (see Researching an Unusual Murder and Canvasing for Witnesses on pg. 34 and 30 respectively). If the player characters missed an opportunity, alternate avenues are available to them. De Lisi has several enemies including many who have seen him use a sonic stunner as a murder weapon. The Sons of Liberty or a Difficult (-2) Streetwise, Soc or Int, 2 days, task can lead the player characters to the following lead:

The Gun Shop is a privately-owned firearm retailer in Liberty's largest shopping district. The proprietor, William Avery, is a Texas immigrant and has owned and operated the store for over a decade. Avery believes in the privacy of his customers and nosy government agents will be met with barely hidden contempt. However a successful Difficult (-2) Persuade Str, Int or Soc check will get Avery to reveal that De Lisi is a regular customer. De Lisi purchased a Brandt Audionique model AS-3 sonic stun pistol from him, which was an unusual choice as most of his customer purchase lethal firearms. De Lisi also visited a month ago to purchase a new power pack and attenuation disc for the stunner.

Finding De Lisi in order to arrest him is as simple as interviewing a confidential informant or a successful Average (+0) Streetwise Soc or Int, 12 hour, check.

De Lisi has no listed home address but spends his free time at Figaro's Boccette Hall in Liberty with his associates, primarily soldiers in the Zagerman Organisation. Use the Bodyguard sample NPC, pg. 85 of the *Traveller Core Rulebook*, and add Deception 1 for De Lisi. De Lisi is accompanied by 1D+1 associates; use the Petty Thug 1 sample NPC, pg. 85, *Traveller Core Rulebook*. De Lisi is carrying an AS-3 sonic stunner and his associates are carrying Hancock 9-23 Enforcers.

Looking for a good time and ready to start trouble, the group has recently ingested Scribble Reds. Their common sense is chemically removed so when the player characters move in to arrest them De Lisi and company will fight back, rather than surrender. The player characters are authorised to use lethal force if need be, though non-lethal restraint would be preferred.

Assuming De Lisi is taken alive, when he sobers he will realise he has no way to get out of his predicament. Loyal to the Zagermans, he will deny any involvement with Si Zagerman or Sonja Kraus but will admit to not only killing Douglas Bailey but Ronald Terrell as well. He will concoct a story about disguising himself as a woman and will provide enough verbal evidence, including the make of the gun and the way Terrell's body fell, to corroborate it. Player characters should make an opposed Carouse or Tactics, Int or Soc check vs. De Lisi's Deception SOC to see through the fabrication.

Taps & Bugs

If the player characters have gathered at least two pieces of evidence linking Beata Rodriguez to Zagerman Organisation activity, AUSA Xander Park will be willing to request an electronic surveillance warrant on Rodriguez. The telecommunications grid on Ellis shares a series of microwave transmission towers which are easily tapped. Voice recognition software will log conversations and provide transcripts of recorded discussions for law enforcement review.

Twenty hours after the tap goes up, the system records an outgoing call from Rodriguez's Link phone requesting a refill. The receiving number is unregistered but a female voice, Sonja Kraus, confirms that the product will arrive at the crew's stash at a specific time of the referee's choosing. If the player characters raided the Spaceport Crew's stash, a new location will have been established. Go to The AmeriCo Connection on pg. 37 if the player characters move to intercept the delivery.

If the player characters have linked Si Zagerman to the Desert Dollhouse, AUSA Park will be willing to request an electronic surveillance warrant on the property. Zagerman and his lieutenants conduct their business in the brothel's VIP lounge at the rear of the building. If the player characters have developed a confidential informant inside the brothel, the informant can be used to visually confirm who makes use of the lounge and any objects of interest, including a large safe secured with a Lv600 (Difficult) electronic lock that Zagerman uses to store his drug money prior to laundering it into his front businesses. The player characters may plant a bug on an informant but the lounge area utilises a privacy-enforcing holofield and the Zagermans have purchased a Momtaro Industries S6 Sensuppress (see pg. 103 *Tools for Frontier Living*). This will foil a TL 12 bug, such as a WitnessWire. Also, it is unlikely the group's leadership will discuss a criminal conspiracy in the presence of an outsider.

An alternate option is to physically plant one or more bugs in the room, then run a filter program to clean up the white noise. The player characters can fake an emergency maintenance call and plant bugs, drill into the room through the wall from the roof or a connecting building or use any other plausible method the referee permits. The player characters will need to make a successful Average (+0) Deception or Recon, Int or Edu, 5 minute, check in order to plant the bugs where Sonja Kraus or another soldier will not detect them. If a confidential informant has scouted the room beforehand, add DM+2. If the player characters fail the check, the bugs are still planted but Sonja Kraus, or another soldier if Kraus is in custody (use Kraus's attributes and Recon skill), may make an opposed Recon, Int check against the player characters' result. If the bugs are found, the organisation leadership will flee to prearranged safe houses across the county and stay out of contact for at least one year.

	Career Path	STR	DEX	END	INT	EDU	SOC
Si Zagerman	Rogue (Enforcer) 2, Rogue (Thief) 2	7	8	10	11	9	9

Deception 1, Gun Combat (slug pistol) 1, Leadership 2, Persuade 1, Stealth 1, Streetwise 2
Traits: Fearless, Vengeful
Equipment: Link phone, Armoured Overcoat, M57 pistol
DNAM: Dry World

	Career Path	STR	DEX	END	INT	EDU	SOC
Edwin LaPlante	Rogue (Enforcer) 1, Rogue (Thief) 3	3	6	7	7	10	10

Advocate 1, Gambler 1, Gun Combat (slug pistol), Leadership 1, Persuade 2, Streetwise 2
Traits: Fast, Hard to Kill
Equipment: Link phone (implant), C4 Wallet Gun
DNAM: Dry World

	Career Path	STR	DEX	END	INT	EDU	SOC
Sonja Kraus	Rogue (Enforcer) 4	7	7	9	7	5	5

Athletics 1, Deception 1, Gun Combat (slug pistol) 2, Recon 1, Shotgun 1, Streetwise 1
Traits: Coolness Under Fire, Tough
Equipment: 9mm (.357 Magnum) pistol, Wildcat Shotgun, Surplus Vest, Link phone
DNAM: Dry World

Note: All three possess High Clubs and Middle Diamond motivations.

If the bugs are successfully planted, the audio data gathered over the course of three days is enough to satisfy AUSA Park. A judge will issue an arrest warrant for the organisation's leadership. Go to The Arrests and Trial on pg. 37.

The AmeriCo Connection

If the player characters witness a resupply of Scribble, they will be surprised to see an AmeriCo truck (use the Utility Van, pg. 174, *2300AD*) arrive at the dealers' stash. Sonja Kraus will open the truck and quickly hand several crates of snack food to the dealers before departing. The snack food bags provide camouflage for the packets of Scribble.

If the player characters follow the truck, they should make an opposed Drive (wheeled), Dex vs. Kraus' Recon, Int check. If the player characters are spotted, Kraus will pull the truck to the side of the road and refuse to move until the player characters leave. If the player characters are not spotted, they will be lead to the AmeriCo packaging plant in Liberty. The truck will proceed through the automated gate and park in the employee lot. From there, Kraus will proceed into the plant where she will remain for 1D+1 hours until another refill is called for.

If the player characters bust Kraus after she leaves from the plant, the characters will find hundreds of doses of Scribble inside the truck along with Kraus's personal firearms. Kraus carries an unregistered Link phone but the only numbers in the system are for the drug crew chiefs. Kraus, Zagerman and LaPlante only meet face-to-face and at prearranged times.

The player characters will be unable to bring the full force of the NSO down upon AmeriCo. If they do so, the company will respond with a full memetic assault, proclaiming its innocence. However the NSO will certainly provide intelligence on AmeriCo's behaviour to the American government. If AmeriCo approaches the government for any sort of partnership or assistance, the government will use this knowledge as leverage.

The Arrests and Trial

Zagerman Leadership: If a combination of Sonja Kraus, Fosco De Lisi and Beata Rodriguez are taken into custody or if the AmeriCo plant is raided, the Zagerman Organisation's lawyer, Erin Cross, will advise Si Zagerman that arrests by law enforcement will be forthcoming. Zagerman and LaPlante will begin to shut down operations. LaPlante will meet with Miyuki Gould at a neutral location and tell her to stop manufacturing Scribble for the time being. Any remaining Scribble product will be sold by the dealers with profits kept by crew chiefs. The money in the Desert Dollhouse safe will be handed over to Erin Cross and kept in a secret account. Enjoying the comforts of the brothel, Zagerman and LaPlante will patiently wait for the player characters to raid the Desert Dollhouse and will not resist.

If the player characters raid the Dollhouse prior to the AmeriCo plant and/or without arresting Kraus, De Lisi and/or Rodriguez, they will find the safe contains nearly Lv1,000,000 in drug money.

In either event, Zagerman and LaPlante will plead guilty to charges of narcotics distribution in order to avoid possible homicide charges. Without the drug money as evidence, the judge will sentence the two men to five years in Federal prison on Earth with a possibility of early parole. If the money is presented as evidence, no early release will be possible.

If Sonja Kraus is linked to the murder of Douglas Bailey, she will plead guilty and be sentenced to life imprisonment on Earth. Otherwise, she will follow Zagerman and LaPlante to Earth for a five year stint.

The Crew: If taken alive, De Lisi will be found guilty on several counts of premeditated homicide and sentenced to mandatory personality wipe.

If Beata Rodriguez is arrested and charged with drug distribution, she will almost relieved. The weight of the cold-blooded murder of Douglas Bailey has driven her into a deep depression. On a successful Difficult (-2) Persuade, Int or Soc check she will confirm that De Lisi murdered Bailey on Kraus's orders. She will gladly accept punishment for her role as a drug distributor but if she cooperates her sentence will be reduced to three years in a Federal prison.

Others: If AmeriCo is traced as the Scribble manufacturer, Miyuki Gould will face her own informal trial before AmeriCo Ellis's senior leadership. Her directors will quietly vote to 'retire' her. Within a few weeks, Gould's personal automobile will mysteriously explode as AmeriCo cleans house.

Desert and Reward

WARNING: IN ORDER TO PRESERVE SUSPENSE, PLAYERS SHOULD READ NO FURTHER. REFEREE'S MATERIAL FOLLOWS.

Adventure Background

Access to water is essential for survival and prosperity on Ellis. The Department of Extraplanetary Resources (USDER) carefully manages the delicate system of desalinisation plants, aqueducts and irrigation canals that feed fresh water from Ellis's remaining lake systems to colonial farms. It is believed that small aquifers, remnants of Ellis's past as a garden world, are hidden across the planet. The US government employs scouts who search for these unseen treasures. However, actual finds are very rare.

Supporters of New America arrived within the first decade of the Ellis colony's founding. The militant group struggled to set up a working base in the planet's arid climate. Stockpiles of water were impossible to come by. With consumption closely monitored, New America could not siphon sufficient amounts from public systems without drawing attention. However, the movement eventually received a break.

After inheriting the family farm on the border of Liberty County, New America regional commander Zachariah Modine discovered that his father had financed a series of private hydrological surveys. The expeditions had focused unclaimed ancient lake beds near the farm but just beyond the county line. The amount of permeable rock is the area was a strong indicator that an ancient aquifer could be nearby. Unfortunately, the elder Modine had died before the drilling was completed. Using the original reports as a guide, Zachariah recruited a small group of trusted sympathisers and continued the survey.

Five years later, Modine's team finally struck a fossil aquifer tucked within the escarpment of a shallow canyon formed by centuries of scouring winds. New America began a covert mining project, hollowing out a labyrinth of tunnels above the aquifer that would serve as a hidden headquarters for the organisation. With a source of water beneath it, the base would be the perfect staging ground for a New America-led uprising.

By 2298, New America realised it had neither the technical knowledge nor the equipment to actually tap the confined aquifer. Modine dispatched a trusted enforcer, Mischa Cadiz, to Meetpoint Station at Sol. At Meetpoint, Cadiz hired the eight employee staff of Mahal & Loke. As a start-up colonial development firm, M&L was desperate for work and happy to take the contract.

Cadiz returned to Ellis in early 2299 with the M&L contingent. Modine convinced M&L that his operation was a start-up mineral extraction company. He insisted the cavern's location and their activities be kept secret from possible competitors and claim-jumpers. M&L agreed to keep the project quiet and the amount of money offered ensured their silence.

By 2300, drilling was completed and a pump system was installed in the aquifer. Modine now had a functioning headquarters but was left with a significant problem. M&L were a liability as they were civilians with working knowledge of New America's Liberty-area secret base. Disposing of them in the vast deserts of Ellis would be easy. However, if the M&L staff did not pass through Boise Spaceport prior to their visas expiring, the federal government would come looking for them. Modine instructed Cadiz to escort M&L through outbound visa processing. He was to then utilise New America's physical assets to ensure the staff disappeared before boarding their ship for Earth.

When it was time for M&L to depart, Cadiz followed the instructions. The M&L employees went through visa processing and Cadiz escorted them to a brief 'goodbye party' at a New America-owned warehouse. There Cadiz and a group of New America muscle killed the eight foreigners by slashing throats and piercing organs with blades. The bodies were stuffed into two large ore sled canisters and the victims' belongings were dropped into spaceport recycling. The ore sled canisters were placed with ore deliveries from Ellis on a delivery dock apron. The intention was to have the canister contents dumped into the station's massive ore storage bins. There they would stay until they were measured into larger loads for outgoing commercial ships. The action of the crushing and shifting ore would grind the bodies until nothing recoverable remained. However, the plan did not succeed.

During a routine security sweep, Ellis State Trooper Jodie Flynn discovered a pair of improperly sealed ore canisters. Upon opening it, she discovered the remains.

The dock apron where the victims' remains were found was staffed by union dockers including Michael Baczkowksi, the International Orbital Dockers Union Chapter 13 secretary-treasurer. Baczkowski was also a veteran smuggler. In order to protect his fellow workers he influenced Ellis politicians with funds gained through his black market activities. His most recent crusade was against the state government's push for a completely automated cargo checking system. While accused of greed by the opposition, Baczkowski's only concern has been the steady employment of his fellow dockers. Robots had already replaced 50% of Boise's original dockers. Those left worried that they could be forced to move back to Ellis or return to unemployment on Earth.

As a smuggler, Baczkowski's only client was Zachariah Modine. Modine paid Baczkowski handsomely to ensure that incoming contraband avoided the eyes of customs inspectors. Baczkowski and his union friend Ermir Leka were responsible for shifting marked cargo from the high-security apron to the low-security apron. This allowed Cadiz and others on Modine's payroll easy access for pick-ups. Baczkowski and Leka preferred not to know what they were slipping past Customs.

On the day of the murders, Cadiz used his warehouse worker's access badge to enter the low-security drop-off area on the Red Section dock apron. This was not unusual. However, rather than stopping, Cadiz used a clone of Ermir Leka's RFID badge to drive the canisters containing the victims into the medium-security ore-delivery area. With the cloned badge, Cadiz hoped to throw law enforcement off of his scent.

The Cast of Desert and Reward

- Ahuja, Diya – Murdered female employee of Mahal & Loke. Age 34.
- Baczkowski, Michael – Local AODU chapter leader and smuggler.
- Cadiz, Mischa – Employee of Zachariah Modine.
- Chandran, Pari – Murdered female employee of Mahal & Loke. Age 30.
- Dekker, Ivan – Docker and member of the AODU.
- Flynn, Sgt. Jodie – Ellis State Police trooper and NSO liaison at Boise.
- Freedman, Dr. Hugh – Ellis State Police medical examiner at Boise.
- Hammet, Eli – Black market reseller living at Boise.
- Hart, Val – Fence and associate of Zachariah Modine.
- Leka, Ermir – Docker, a close associate of Michael Baczkowksi and a member of the AODU.
- Loke, Saanvi – Murdered female employee of Mahal & Loke. Age 41.
- Mahal, Purno – Murdered male employee of Mahal & Loke. Age 44.
- Modine, Zachariah – New America regional commander.
- Mukherjee, Aanya – Murdered female employee of Mahal & Loke. Age 29.
- Pileggi, Dean – Fence, owner of Big Pig Warehousing and Zachariah Modine's representative at Boise Spaceport.
- Ramachandran, Suravaram – Murdered male employee of Mahal & Loke. Age 33.
- Singh, Pranab – Murdered male employee of Mahal & Loke. Age 40.
- Sura, Mohammad – Murdered male employee of Mahal & Loke. Age 25.
- Wan, Samuel – Drug dealer at Boise Spaceport.

The Briefing

At the beginning of the adventure, the player characters are roused from their beds. A high-priority message from the NSO field office request that they report to Liberty Spaceport at 06:00 for immediate departure to Boise. When they arrive at the spaceport they are hustled aboard their waiting transport. Transit through Ellis's highly-charged Van Allen belts exposes a standard spacecraft to toxic levels of ionizing radiation. The craft the player characters board is a modified *Hayabusa*-class transport that has been heavily reinforced with both passive and active shielding systems. As the transport crew conducts its pre-flight operations, SSA Karli Kapinos runs a secured virtual Link briefing.

'I apologise for the rush,' Kapinos begins. 'The office received an urgent referral from the Ellis State Police. You're being dispatched to take immediate control of a crime scene.

'At 03:20 Boise Spaceport Time, a Transportation Authority Service trooper discovered the remains of eight bodies in a pair of ore canisters. The victims had multiple puncture and slashing wounds. There was no identification on the victims but biometrics matched the remains to employees of Mahal & Loke of Bombay. According to Customs, they passed through on work visas in March of last year. Their visas were sponsored by ZM Enterprises, a small resource extraction and virtual start-up incorporated in Liberty. I did a check on ZM Enterprises and it appears to be a dummy front. It has filed no taxes and their business license is an electronic forgery.

'The victims passed through Customs again at 16:45 yesterday. According to their itinerary they were to board the transport Houston Again *for their trip back to Earth. They missed their board-call at 19:20 and the ship left without them.*

'Your case assignment is to determine who was responsible for the victims' deaths, find out why and provide Assistant US Attorney Xander Park enough evidence for a successful prosecution. If the need for electronic surveillance arises, Park will assist in securing a warrant.'

Possible Questions and Answers

Why isn't the state police investigating this crime?

'The victims are foreign nationals and the number of victims is beyond the capacity of the state police. Those two factors combined make it a federal case.'

What do we know about Mahal & Loke and the victims?

'The eight victims were the entirety of the Mahal & Loke staff. The company was a fresh new start-up based on Meetpoint Station and was actively soliciting for off-world business. They advertised themselves as "colonial resource and infrastructure development consultants." There are over a hundred of these small Pathfinder outfits operating across Ellis. If locals have the funds to hire partners but lack the equipment or expertise, they will often bring in one of these companies to survey a mining site, build habitats or even lay roads or tracks.'

What is the Bombay government's response?

'The victims were discovered yesterday. Our local State Department attaché is still crafting a response to send to Earth. From there, State will contact the Bombay embassy. It will be weeks if not months before we receive any formal requests from them.'

What equipment are we bringing with us?

See the Equipment List on pg. 41.

Do you have any leads or any additional information about the victims for us?

'Not at this time. Talk to the state police when you arrive at the spaceport.'

The Investigation

Like Profit Without Honour, Desert and Reward is not a linear adventure. Players may begin with the leads they have and follow them however they choose. Careful observation, deduction and informants will all play an important part in the investigation. SSA Kapinos remains available for advice. If the player characters contact her by radio from Boise, there will be a manageable 56 second radio transmission delay as Boise's current orbit places it at 17 million kilometres distance from Ellis. If the player characters want to use electronic surveillance, AUSA Park will determine if they have done enough work to warrant it.

Desert and Reward is technically in two parts. In the first part, the player characters deduce who was responsible for the murders. Once the actual perpetrators are identified, the player characters will lead an assault on New America's Liberty base of operations.

Referees should note that some dates and times for events in this adventure are exact in order to preserve verisimilitude where other time spans are left open for interpretation. Unless otherwise noted, referees are free to be as strict or as loose with the passage of time as fits the tone of the story and the interests of players.

Equipment List

The NSO has provided the player characters with the following equipment in addition to their standard side-arms.

2 AuraOptika laser ears
3 cable taps
1 electronic security system kit
1 forensics kit
1 box of glowsticks
1 pair goggles per player character
1 hand torch per player character
1 pair heavy boots per player character
1 pair heavy gloves per player character
1 HotShot imager
1 locksmith kit
2 makeup kits
1 encrypted microcomm per player character
1 NSO baseball cap per player character
1 NSO cheap jacket per player character
1 box of 6 Odonata improved bugs
1 portacomp with encrypted government Link access and decryption software per player character
2 boxes of 25 government-issue radio frequency ID tags
1 box of 10 green Stick-Kit patches

Schematics of Boise have been uploaded to the player characters' Link phones. Player characters are authorised to requisition equipment and space, such as interview rooms, from the state police post at Boise if needed. However, referees should limit what the troopers provide to non-lethal weapons, restraints, gas grenades, shotguns, light armour and skinsuits.

The player characters are assigned an apartment suite for their stay at Boise. While the suite is not luxurious, it contains a comfortable common room with kitchen and each player character will have a private bedroom and bath. Meals and other incidentals will be compensated for by the NSO so long as the player characters are not spending money in an extravagant fashion. If the player characters are eating beefalope steaks for every dinner, the NSO will refuse to issue a refund. As Boise is a working spaceport and only a draw for military personnel based in Oyster orbit, the temptation will be mitigated.

Boise

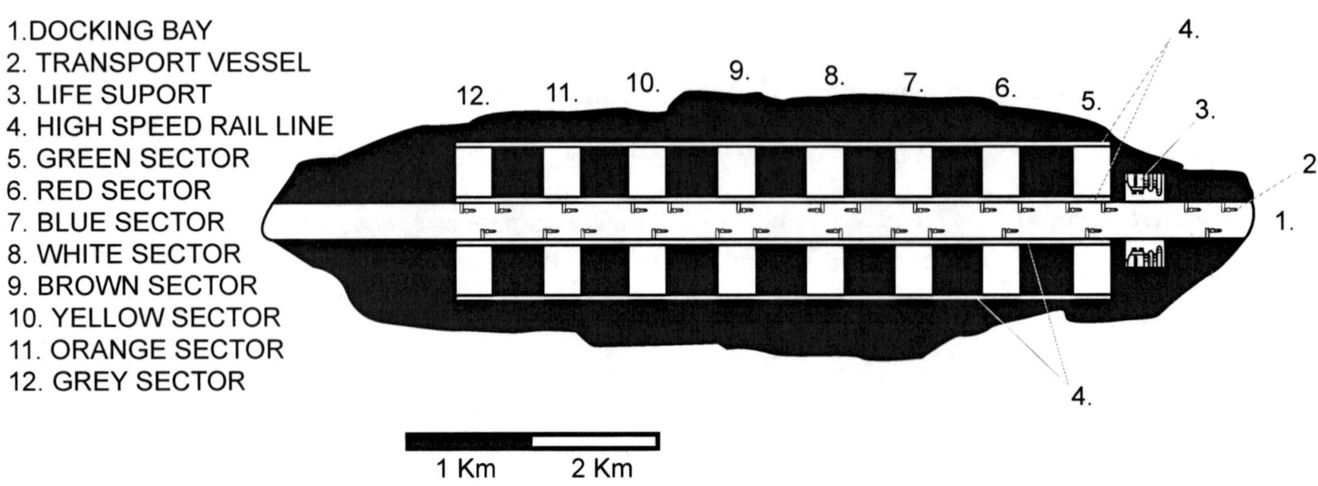

Prior to Boise Spaceport's construction, the Ellis colony was served by drop pods and limited runs of standard interface shuttles. The planet's highly charged Van Allen belt was a radiation hazard for orbiting spacecraft. The ionised radiation also prevented the construction of a permanent orbital terminal. If the colony was going to be an economically viable enterprise, an alternate option was needed.

A suitable construction site was identified in 2249. Boise, an 8 × 2 kilometre M-type asteroid located in Oyster's L5 trojan point, was considered ideal. The asteroid's form would allow for artificial gravity with minimal wobble and its ample mass provided material feedstock for future expansion.

Several experimental techniques were proposed for the rapid development of Boise, ranging from wrapping the asteroid in a polymer sheath and spinning the body after melting it with a solar mirror to filling it with water that would then be flash vaporised to quickly hollow it. These techniques proved to be too energy intensive or risked cracking the asteroid. While more time intensive, the traditional drill method, perfected from decades of application in Sol's Belt, was finally settled upon by the Port Authority.

The US Army Corps of Engineers commenced boring the central core shaft in 2250. The 300 metre-wide, 8 kilometre-long docking port, running from fore to the aft of the asteroid, would be capable of comfortably accommodating the largest commercial vessels. Utilising private sector sub-contractors, habitat tunnels were cleared in 2258. A 0.2 RPM spin was introduced in order to aid workers installing life support systems. As construction continued, Boise eventually settled into 0.6 RPM. This resulted in a comfortable 0.8 G environment in the middle rim of the asteroid with the docking port remaining in microgravity. Sensors and traffic control systems were installed in the outer rim and in 2270 the spaceport was opened.

Pilots approaching Boise match the docking core's slight rotation with station-keeping thrusters and enter the spaceport's 'north' end. Departing vessels exit through the 'south' egress. Spinward on the asteroid is designated as 'west' in station-parlance and anti-spinward is 'east'. The dock complex itself is an 8 kilometre tube of gantries, umbilical lines, grapplers, derricks, cranes, lifts, repair bays and airlocks. The docking port runs the length of the asteroid but barely a quarter of the asteroid's internal volume has been cleared.

Habitat and life support space is primarily located at the north end of the asteroid. Warehousing, ore bins and industrial space run the length of the inner core, just below the docks. Automated high-speed rail cars and elevators move passengers, residents and cargo canisters from one end of the spaceport to the other. The spaceport utilises the common habitat scheme of colour-coding sections. For ease of navigation, public corridor walls and signage in each section are painted with its assigned section colour. Beginning at the north end of the spaceport are the primary habitat areas: Green Section, followed by Red Section. The following sections are primarily docks and warehousing: Blue, White, Brown, Yellow, Orange and Grey. Residential construction is scheduled to begin in Blue Section in 2301.

Boise Spaceport's designers developed the asteroid's habitat spaces for long-term residency. Public area ceilings are illuminated with reflected sunlight from the asteroid's solar mirror array. Planters with various species of decorative flowers are placed in manicured alcoves and both Red and Green Section have large green spaces for resident enjoyment as well as oxygen production. All thoroughfare walls are lined with panels of muted, natural colours found in soil and trees or LED screens running news or announcements. Residences are smaller than what would be found on a planet's surface but are larger than most space stations. Occupants are given reasonable latitude when it comes to decoration and residences reflect their occupant's taste.

The Boise Spaceport Authority (BSA) employs over 4000 full-time employees who are permanently assigned to the asteroid. Various employee support service industries employ an additional 1,900 people. Approximately 2,500 individuals make use of the temporary lodging suites available for those transiting in- and out-system. The Inferno, a cluster of hotels, bars, shops and entertainment facilities just off the docks in Red Section, serve the ships' crews and military personnel on leave that call on Boise. Locals typically avoid fraternising with military and commercial spacers, claiming their own bars in Green Section. Non-residents who cross into Green risk starting a fight.

The BSA is headquartered in Liberty with a remote office at Boise. The Ellis governor nominates BSA members to the Authority's twelve-person Board of Commissioners. Board members are then confirmed by the Ellis state senate. The board selects a chair and vice-chair who oversee day-to-day operations from the Boise office. The current chair and vice-chair are both Popular Conservative party members. Neil Brezenoff, the chair, was a vice-president at Trilon prior to being nominated for service. He plans to return to Trilon when his term expires in 2302. Rosanne Goldstein, the vice-chair, was an influential manager at Asterbank and a state representative who served in Congress until a primary election defeat in 2297.

The Ellis State Police Transportation Authority Service serves as station security and ensures that all laws and regulations are obeyed. Individuals caught tampering with station life support or airlock mechanisms are dealt with in a swift and lethal fashion. Civilians are prohibited from keeping firearms or any type of incendiary devices on their person but large utility knives and cargo hooks, common in a spaceport community, are permitted. TAS troopers are specially trained in riot containment and vacuum and microgravity rescue operations. The state police post commander is Major Peter Lindsey, a 20-year veteran of the state troopers.

External defence of Boise is the charge of the United States Space Force. Based out of Oyster Orbit Space Force Base at the L4 asteroid Kellogg, the 1,000-person 15th Wing supports Boise through the maintenance of hunter-killer satellites as well as manned patrols. Military satellites are made up of point defence lasers, rail guns and missile batteries as well as command-and-control shacks. Positioned in defensive clusters, they protect the entirety of Boise's 4,000,000 spherical kilometre airspace.

Reconnaissance flights by JVF-22B and FS-17A space/orbit fighters monitor Oyster's system of asteroids, moons and moonlets for piracy and other threats. Space Force flights also provide security for customs inspectors operating on Boise's flight path. Libertine and unscheduled foreign registry vessels receive extra attention from these pilots.

USSF pilots are typical military aviators; highly trained, patriotic and arrogant. They openly mock other militaries for their use of naval terminology in their space forces. They also maintain a heated rivalry with the Marines stationed on Charlton, who the Spacers claim are unintelligent and muscle-bound jarheads. The Marines view the Spacers as elitist snobs and cowards who shoot down enemies from behind planetary curves rather than face-to-face. The Ellis State Police ramp up trooper patrols in public recreation areas when both Spacers and Marines are on leave at Boise. The current commander of the 15th Wing is General Jane Duvall. Duvall pays respectful deference to General O'Dea at AMARMCOM at Fort Patton.

Evidence of a Crime

The player characters are met at the airlock by Sgt. Jodie Flynn upon arrival at Boise Spaceport. Flynn will serve as the player characters with the Ellis State Police. Use the sample Detective NPC on pg. 84 of the *Traveller Core Rulebook* for Sgt. Flynn and any other Ellis State Trooper. She is a short Caucasian woman in her late 30s with reddish-brown hair and a demure attitude. As she is intimately familiar with the state of the spaceport, referees should use Flynn as friendly source for player character advice and guidance during the investigation.

After a short elevator ride 'down,' the player characters leave microgravity and arrive at the Red Section dock apron. The state police have sealed the scene of the crime. Flynn explains to the player characters what they are seeing. The scene is a 6,096 square-metre space dedicated to incoming ore canisters. To the south of the space is the Red Section dock high-security cargo area, where Customs officials visually inspect incoming bulk cargo. To the north is the low-security cargo area where outgoing cargo waits to be transferred to a ship. The victims' remains were found in the medium-security area which is dedicated to ore deliveries. The victims were found stuffed inside a pair of typical American-standard ore canisters. The canisters are a type that are fitted into a catapult sled prior to be launched from the surface of Ellis. After being staged on the apron, the sealed ore canisters are moved by gantry cranes onto conveyors that carry the canisters to the spaceport's ore bins. Outside the bins, the canisters are unsealed and emptied into the bins for storage. When a bulk carrier ship makes call, ore is shifted from the ore bins into much larger interstellar ore shipping canisters. Those canisters are then loaded onto the ship.

Flynn explains that, for safety compliance, state police troopers make random sweeps of the aprons to ensure that canisters are properly sealed. Otherwise, the canisters risk opening and dumping their loads. This would require a time-intensive and costly clean-up. It was during her third-shift check of the apron when she noticed the first unsealed canister. Opening it to check that the contents were not ready to spill, she discovered the remains of four adult men and women. She immediately found another unsealed canister with a similarly grisly cargo.

The bodies of the victims were removed from the canister by spaceport medics and are now on the dock apron floor. Each victim has been sealed in a transparent polymer body bag. Dr. Hugh Freedman, the Ellis State Police medical examiner at Boise, stands nearby. Freedman is a gangly African-American whose analytical behaviour contrasts with the large hair haloing his head. Freedman tells the player characters that he has done a cursory examination. The victims all have large puncture wounds along the spines and chest and cuts on hands and arms. The cuts indicate defensive wounds and the punctures correspond to a combat knife or large utility tool. The punctures are all in the upper chest/upper back area, indicating the killers knew where to hit vital organs. The bodies were still in a state of rigor when discovered indicating they were killed between 17:00 and 19:00 hours yesterday.

Flynn tells the player characters that none of the victims' personal effects were found in the canister. They presumably had luggage but at this point it could be anywhere on the station. At this point referees should have the player characters make a Simple (+6), Int or Edu check. On a success, the player characters will realise the killers have most likely dumped the victims' possessions into a disposal or recycling bin. If the player characters ask Flynn about it, she will direct the characters to the Red Section central waste reclamation facility. Go to Dumpster Diving.

The Ellis State Police have no suspects at this time and Flynn does not know how the bodies would have been loaded into an ore canister without anyone noticing. Utility corridors are the only areas of the station that are unmonitored but, other than security and station managers, the only people who are authorised to access them are dock workers. If the player characters approach the dockers, go to First Confrontation on pg. 45.

Dumpster Diving

Non-toxic dry waste at the spaceport is deposited into a number of public receptacles. From there they are shunted to a recycling facility through a series of simple pneumatic tubes. Waste is stored in large collection bins prior to processing. Belts move the waste and sort automatically into metals, plastics, food refuse and other materials. Waste entering the collection bin usually sits for 24 hours before being sorted, so if the player characters move quickly, they can find the victims' possessions.

The bins are accessed from the top through a maintenance hatch. They are also pitch black and filled with the stench of rotting food. The smell is technically harmless but overpowering. Player characters without a filter mask will suffer DM-1 on all checks.

On a successful Average (+0) Athletics, End or Str, 1 hour, check, the player characters recover several sets of sealed personal luggage corresponding to the victims. Other than clothing, personal identification, personal items and Hindu and Muslim religious paraphernalia, the player characters discover the following in the luggage cases:

- An e-paper instruction booklet for the Trilon TRj20 Industrial Water Pump detailing proper operation and maintenance.
- Encrypted portacomps with Mahal & Loke company decals affixed to them.
- A sketchbook of landscape drawings labelled 'Property of Pari Chandran' in Hindi. They are primarily doodles of Ellis's terrain: rocks, low hills and ravines.

If the player characters attempt to access one or more of the portacomps, they will need to make a successful Difficult (-2) Computer, Edu or Int, 30 minute, check. The portacomps each contain extremely complicated proprietary geological modelling programs and control algorithms for automated drilling platforms. The portacomps also contain satellite imaging, geological history texts and survey reports concerning the geological makeup of several large stretches of land just east of Liberty County on Ellis. On a successful Average (+0) Science (planetology), Edu check the player characters recognise the various charts and models as corresponding to a water extraction procedure.

A successful Easy (+4) Mechanic, Int or Edu, or an Average (+0) Investigate, Int check will reveal that the TRj20 is a Trilon-manufactured heavy-duty water pump specifically designed to prevent dust and fines from entering moving parts. If the player characters follow up on the pump by contacting the manufacturer on Ellis, a successful Average (+0) Deception, Soc or a Difficult (-2) Persuade, Soc check will reveal that eight TRj20 models were ordered and paid for by a Mr. Purno Mahal eight months ago. They were delivered to a warehouse in Liberty and signed for by a Mr. Suravaram Ramachandran one month later. If the player characters follow up with the warehouse manager, a successful Routine (+2) Persuade, Soc check will confirm that Mahal & Loke rented a space for a week to take delivery of some large machinery. The machinery was loaded into two large and wheeled cargo trucks after being delivered. The manager tells the player characters that M&L was a group of core world Indian sub-continent types. However, the truck drivers were definitely locals and were very tough looking in appearance.

Pari Chandran was a talented amateur artist and liked drawing in her free time. While the sketchbook itself contains no direct clues, it will add DM+2 to attempts to identify the location of the New America command centre as the drawings contain identifiable landmarks.

First Confrontation

If the player characters choose to investigate the docks, Flynn will escort them into Boise's microgravity core. Note that player characters without the Zero-G skill will suffer DM-2 on all skill checks. The supervising dock worker for Red Section is Ermir Leka, a short and large-bellied man in his mid-50s. When the player characters show their identification, Leka turns from mildly curious to stone faced. He will refuse to answer questions or assist the player characters in any way. He will also inform them that he is not obligated to assist them. If the player characters make a successful Difficult (-2) Advocate, Int check they will realise that Leka is hiding behind his union. If they arrest Leka or attempt to coerce him, they will have to face an International Orbital Dockers Union lawyer.

If the player characters want to pursue the union further, they should make an Average (+0) Investigate, Edu or Soc, 1 hour, check. On a success they will discover there have been rumours and allegations of contraband such as drugs and weapons passing through the docks under union eyes. There is a growing drug problem at Boise and it is suspected that the docks may be the source of illegal narcotics.

On a Routine (+2) Carouse, Soc check, the player characters learn that Michael Baczkowski, the AODU secretary-treasurer and several other union dockers, drink at the The Bawdy Lass bar in Green Section. If the player characters visit The Bawdy Lass, go to Second Confrontation.

If the player characters research the union itself, go to The IODU on pg. 45.

If the player characters look into Michael Baczkowski, go to The Secretary-Treasurer on pg. 46.

If the player characters decide to identify the IODU as a target and engage in active surveillance, go to Under Scrutiny on pg. 46.

Second Confrontation

The Bawdy Lass is a raucous local bar in Green Sector with a patronage consisting primarily of dockers. The music is loud and the station-crafted beer, a rare luxury item on Ellis itself, flows freely. Michael Baczkowski can be found in the bar during most of his off-hours. He is usually flanked by his two closest friends, Ivan Dekker and Ermir Leka. Baczkowski appears to be in his late mid-to-late-50s. Though his curly hairline has long since receded and some of his muscle has turned to fat, he is built like an ox and has a matching demeanour. Ivan Dekker appears to be in his early 30s. He is tall and conventionally handsome with dark swept hair. The player characters can attempt to question Baczkowski at the union hall but they will suffer DM-2 on Soc skill checks for approaching him in his seat of power.

No one in the bar will become violent with the player characters but they will sit and fume quietly over law enforcement interrupting their drinks. If the player characters question Baczkowski about the dead bodies found on the Red Section dock apron, he will claim complete ignorance as to how the bodies got there or who would have killed the victims. He did not see anything unusual the day of the murders. A successful Average (+0) Social Sciences (psychology), Soc or Edu check will reveal that he is telling the truth.

If the player characters ask who would have access to the dock apron area, they should make a successful Very Difficult (-4) Persuade, Soc or Str check. On success, Baczkowski will tell them that only dockers, Boise Spaceport management and station security have RFID access badges that permit access to the dock aprons. However the player characters will have a strong suspicion that Baczkowksi, while telling the truth, is not telling them the complete story.

At the end of the conversation, Baczkowski will growl that the player characters, 'are just like every other union-busting cop looking to sully our good name.'

The IODU

Success on a Simple (+6) Informatics, Edu or Easy (+4) Advocate, Edu or Int check will reveal that the International Orbital Dockers Union was organised in 2223 in response to unsafe working conditions at Hyde Dynamics's He3 collection facility in Lunar orbit. In an effort to boost shareholder profits, Hyde introduced cost-cutting measures that including the installation of aftermarket life support systems in off-planet facilities. When a catastrophic mechanical failure resulted in the venting of nine unprotected dock workers, employees in all of Hyde's orbital habitats chose to strike.

Rather than negotiating, Hyde launched security teams from Earth with orders to forcibly retake the properties. These boarders were met by angry dockers armed with construction tools. In what came to be known in popular culture as 'The Battle of Luna,' 13 Hyde employees were killed and 57 more were wounded. When the TransNat faced a loss of public support, Hyde management pulled its forces and reached out to the strikers' leader, Samantha V. Robins. After three days of radio negotiations, Hyde agreed to exclusive worker control of its orbital facilities.

The Battle of Luna led to labourers in habitats across the Sol system organising into what would eventually be the International Orbital Dockers Union in 2249. Many Earth governments and TransNats recognised the union's legitimacy but others did not. Both Trilon and AmeriCo became adept at union-busting and employees caught fraternising with union reps were threatened with sanctions under corporate law.

The IODU's fall from grace began in 2278 when the union was linked to labour racketeering through several Manchurian Triads. Evidence of rigged union elections and exploited worker funds called the entire organisation into question. The American government, with its anti-labour Popular Conservative-dominated leadership, opened a series of probes into the IODU's American chapters. The corrupt practices were primarily limited to the Chinese Arm but corporate lobbyists insisted the union open all of its bank accounts to public scrutiny. The IODU as a whole was eventually exonerated of wrong-doing but the TransNats' memetic assaults were successful. Its reputation tainted, IODU membership shrank. As of 2300, the IODU is at 40% of its strength from its height in the 2250s. The IODU leadership considers the NSO and other government agencies tools of the TransNats; it is typically hostile toward them. The election of a leftist-leaning American Party candidate to the US Presidency is the first sign of hope the union has seen in decades.

The IODU Local Chapter 13 was present at Boise when the spaceport opened in 2270. It maintains a meeting hall in Red Section. The five room hall consists of a large convocation area, where a large portrait of Samantha Robins hangs on the back wall, and offices for union leaders. The union chapter leader's title is that of Secretary-Treasurer and is responsible for overseeing the chapter's finances. The position is obtained by a simple majority vote. The current secretary-treasurer, Michael Baczkowski, has served for seven years and plans to run again.

Counter to TransNat and conservative propaganda, the life of a docker is not an easy one. Boise dockers run heavy gantry cranes and exo-loaders along with orbital transfer vehicles that gather catapult sleds launched from Ellis. The high turn-around speed for loading and unloading cargoes and the incredibly heavy and dangerous equipment involved is a recipe for accidents. Crushed and severed limbs, along with vacuum related injuries and deaths, are not unheard of. Dockers have two dominant sub-cultures: the 'stevedores' who move cargo to and from the docks and the 'shepherds' who retrieve and deliver catapult sleds to the docks. The two maintain a playful rivalry.

If the player characters make a successful Average (+0) Broker, Edu, 10 min, check they will find through examining the union's publicly available books that union membership is on the decline and the local chapter has been having difficulties paying its debts. However, the union has been making financial contributions to several pro-union political candidates which indicates it has an alternate source of funding.

The Secretary-Treasurer

The Ellis State Police post has several files on the union, mostly complaints about missing valuable luxury items from the Core, such as spirits or personal electronics. None of the investigations have borne fruit and no dockers have admitted to wrong-doing, though many will admit that items occasionally 'fall out of a container.'

On a successful, Average (+0) Investigate, Int or Soc, 2 days, check the player characters will learn that Michael Baczkowski has served as the leader of the local IODU chapter for 14 years. Now age 59, Baczkowski was born on Ellis to Liberty Spaceport employee parents and was employed as a checker by age 20. He was among the first batch of dockers hired at Boise when the spaceport came online in 2270. He ran for secretary-treasurer in 2286 and won a sweeping majority.

Baczkowski is known as a man who takes care of his people. If a docker is injured on the job, he makes sure the person is given the best possible medical treatment. If a docker is killed, the family will have what it needs. No docker is rich but no docker needs for anything.

He is preparing for another run at union leadership but is running into pushback from some of the union members. Ivan Dekker, a charismatic docker in his early 30s, sees the election of an American Party president as a positive sign and wants to end the unspoken 'war' between the union and the corporations/government. Baczkowski believes Dekker is naïve and that corporate voices for more dock-side automation are driven by profits rather than concerns about worker safety.

He is married with two adult sons.

Under Scrutiny

With Baczkowski and the IODU as their only lead, the player characters should be motivated to observe the group. The player characters have three options to explore:

- Drugs are smuggled through spaceports. If the player characters can identify dealers and follow the supply train it may lead back to the union. If the player characters pursue this lead, go to The Vice Trade.
- Sales of cargo stolen from docks as well as black market items take place in what are called undermarkets. Hosted by fences in unoccupied warehouses, these temporary fire sales move stolen goods and contraband into the hands of pirates, small-time smugglers and Libertines. Stolen items may lead back to the union. If the player characters pursue this lead, go to The Undermarket on pg. 47.

- If the player characters want to investigate how smuggling may work, go to Following the Canisters on pg. 48.

The Vice Trade

It is reasonable to believe that contraband at Boise filters through the docks at some point. Drug deals at the spaceport are discreet but it is a thriving industry. If the player characters plan to watch the drug trade and follow it up the ladder, they can begin by investigating the local dealers. A successful Average (+0) Streetwise, Soc or Int check will put the player characters on to Samuel Wan, a short-order cook and manager at the Starlight Diner in Green Section. Wan supplements his income at the diner by selling small packages of Scribble under the table to spaceport workers.

If the player characters want to bug Wan's Link or apartment they will need to acquire an electronic surveillance warrant. However, player characters are free to simply observe his movements, use electronic surveillance in a public environment, such as the diner, or even do hand-to-hand drug buys.

If the player characters simply observe Wan, they learn the following on a successful Simple (+4) Recon, End or Int, 2D days, check: Wan has a regular clientele of about a dozen spaceport workers though he will also sell to spacer crews passing through. Wan only sells to buyers who have been referred to him by other users. He knows an individual has been referred if a new buyer asks him if the rat meat omelettes are fresh. Rat omelettes were discontinued years ago. Deals will always occur in the back office of the diner, to avoid snooping eyes.

If the player characters want to bust Wan for dealing, they will need to do a buy-bust. If they know the passphrase, a successful Routine (+2) Deception, Soc check will get them into Wan's tiny office. Once drugs are in hand, the player characters can arrest him if they choose.

Once the player characters have Wan in a state police interview room, he will spill what he knows with a successful Routine (+2) Persuade, Str or Soc check. Go to The Manufacturer on pg. 50 Alternately, the player characters can shadow Wan. On a successful Difficult (-2) Stealth, Dex or Int, 3 days, check the player characters observe Wan taking a rail shuttle to Orange Section. There, the player characters see Wan enter a secondary corridor away from the main warehouses and into a pre-fab construction module, the kind used by engineers and managers when overseeing drilling new habitat space in the asteroid. The module is guarded by two, rather large construction workers. Go to The Manufacturer on pg. 50.

The Undermarket

Undermarkets are the black market equivalent of shopping bazaars. These invitation-only events are set up in empty, out of the way spaces in or near spaceports. By the time law enforcement realises an event is taking place, the undermarket quickly breaks down and goes into hiding until a new location is secured.

The current 'madam' of the Boise Undermarket is Val Hart. A veteran fence, she receives a cut of all sales by making sure black market sellers are able to conduct their business. Not only does she employ the physical security for these bazaars, she conducts informal screenings of new customers.

The easiest way for the player characters to gain access to the Boise Undermarket is to find a regular patron and flip him. A successful Routine (+2) Streetwise, Soc, 1 day or Difficult (-2) Investigate, Soc or Int, 3 days check will lead the player characters to Eli Hammett. Hammet is a former pirate scout and was stranded at Boise when his shipmates were arrested by the authorities. Taking day jobs when he can find them, he supplements his income as a black market reseller by purchasing goods at the Undermarket and peddling them to whoever has money.

If the player characters take Hammet in for interrogation they should make an Average (+0) Persuade Soc or Str check. A success will result in Hammet providing the player characters with the proper Link number, Val's name and description and protocols for new shoppers at the Undermarket.

The player characters will first need to call Val Hart's unregistered Link and pass a short interview. A successful Simple (+2) Deception, Soc or Int check will keep Hart's suspicions at bay. She will arrange for a liaison to meet them the following day at the Food Extruder kiosk in the Green Section Restaurant Row.

At the time and location of the meet, two large males wearing conservative attire will approach the player characters. Use the Petty Thug sample NPC from pg. 84 of the *Traveller Core Rulebook* and arm each with a dagger. They will ask the player characters to raise their arms and submit to a search.. They will not answer questions or make conversation. Weapons will be confiscated and at the sign of any large recording devices, they will inform the player characters that their business is concluded. If the player characters use Implanted or small bugs the two enforcers will overlook them.

Once the pat-down is complete, the player characters will be escorted to a rail transit station. Boarding a rail car, they will travel south to Yellow Section Station where they disembark. Travelling on foot, they arrive at a locked warehouse service door in a side corridor. Guarded by another pair of humourless enforcers, these two outwardly brandish Wildcat shotguns (pg. 112, *Tools for Frontier Living*).

UNDERMARKET WAREHOUSE

1. OVERHEAD DOOR
2. STALLS
3. FOYER
4. OFFICE
5. MEETING ROOM
6. WASHROOMS

3 METRES

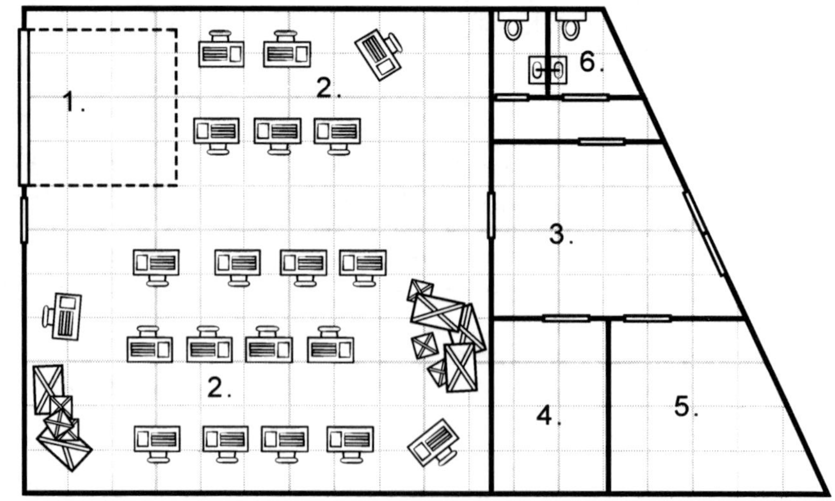

Beyond the door is the Undermarket. Consisting of 20 stalls, black market dealers hawk the usual weapons, pornography and drugs along with stolen consumer goods including electronics, designer clothes, jewellery and house drones. Even alcohol and tobacco products are for sale, though at a fraction of standard market prices. Approximately 150 random shoppers, ranging from corporate managers to dockers to local farmers to off-duty military personnel, haggle with vendors.

Val Hart has set herself up in the warehouse manager's office which overlooks the scene from the gantry level above. She has no set schedule and leaves at random hours, accompanied by her enforcers, to return to her apartment in Green Section. Access to the office is limited to a winding metal staircase, guarded by three armed enforcers. Four additional enforcers wander the floor ensuring that everyone behaves themselves. The warehouse is the ideal location for a black market bazaar as the exposed metal support structure combined with the metallic rock composition of Boise defeats most wireless radio signals. Player characters attempting to monitor activities remotely will need to either make appropriate modifications to listening devices prior the meeting, requiring a successful Average (+0) Physical Science (electronics), Int, 2 hours check, or will need to succeed on a Very Difficult (-4) Sensors, Int or Edu check to adjust the bugs on-the-fly.

Referees should encourage players to think carefully about how to approach the situation. Ideally, only one or two player characters would actually go undercover. The remaining player characters may remain behind to monitor the situation and storm the Undermarket when the target is identified.

Once the player characters make their move on Hart, the shoppers and sellers will attempt to flee the scene. The main warehouse door will be flung open and the occupants will stream out. For the first three rounds of combat, all participants will suffer DM-2 as bodies shove into other bodies. Barring the doors will result in deaths as shoppers are crushed against bulkheads or are trampled in a panic. Referees who want to make it easy on players may have the player characters make a Difficult (-2) Recon, Int check. On a success, the player characters will spot Hart leaving from her office after a long day and may attempt to follow her.

Once arrested, player characters may attempt to interview Hart though she will demand the presence of her lawyer. A successful Very Difficult (-4) Diplomat, Soc or Int check will convince Hart to hold off on a lawyer. If successful, an Average (+0) Persuade, Soc check will get her to spill what she knows. If the player characters fail their Diplomat check, getting Hart to open up will require a successful Difficult (-2) Advocate, Int or Soc check to negotiate past her lawyer.

Assuming the player characters are successful, Hart will share what she knows about her part in the criminal conspiracy. She will reveal that she is part of a larger group operating at Boise. This conspiracy includes one or more union dockers (she does not know specifically who) and Big Pig Warehousing in Red Section which is owned by Dean Pileggi. She knows that Pileggi is in direct contact with an individual on Ellis who directly oversees their financial compensation. She does not know who the individual is but she suspects he may be a political radical.

If they follow up on Big Pig Warehousing, go to pg. 52.

Following the Canisters

In order to understand how the dock system works, the player characters will need to ingratiate themselves to one of the dockers working in Red Section. Sgt. Flynn will introduce the player characters to Ivan Dekker, assuming the player characters did not meet him at The Bawdy Lass (see Second Confrontation on pg. 45). Dekker maintains a quiet crush towards Flynn and will agree to cooperate with the player characters if she asks him to.

Dekker will escort the player characters to the Red Section dock operations centre. The office consists of a handful of workstations and large data projections signifying where cargo canisters are located.

Dekker explains how cargo moves on the docks as follows:

1. Incoming freight arrives at the spaceport aboard a cargo ship or, in the case of ore sleds from Ellis, in tow behind an orbital transfer vehicle driven by a shepherd.
2. Using a combination of exo-rigs with magnetic foot clamps, gantry cranes and elevators, freight is moved from the berthed space vehicle in microgavity 'down' to the dock apron. As the freight is unloaded from the ship, the manifest mounted on the canister is scanned by an automated reader. That data is recorded in the dock inventory.
3. When freight arrives at the warehouse level it is sorted into three groups on the apron:
    a. Freight headed out-system is moved from its warehouse to the low-security apron. Customs and security ignore this area. If a canister is not headed for Ellis, it is not their problem.
    b. Natural resource canisters from Ellis, typically ore or petroleum, are moved to the medium-security apron. The valuable and hazardous nature of this cargo demands moderate safety and security measures.
    c. Incoming freight is moved to the high-security apron where Customs inspectors examine canisters and confirm manifests.
4. On the apron, all canisters are manually checked and confirmed by stevedores to ensure they are placed in the right section.
5. Natural resource canisters are moved via gantry crane and conveyor to nearby storage where the canisters are emptied into massive bins. When an empty ship calls on the dock, outgoing materials are deposited directly into its waiting holds via conveyor.
6. Incoming freight from out-system, after clearing Customs inspection, is moved to an assigned warehouse.

If the player characters ask Dekker to pull up the manifest records for the canisters the victims' bodies were found in, he will do so. He will then say;

'That's odd. Those canister numbers aren't in our incoming shipment inventory. But the reader does sometimes malfunction and miss canisters on their way down to the apron. It says here that Ermir Leka checked it in. On occasion canisters get placed on the wrong aprons upon arrival. They get shifted to the right place and reconfirmed. That's why we stevedores are employed.'

If the player characters would like to remotely monitor the dock inventory system, they will need to approach the dock administrator. On a successful Easy (+4) Advocate, Soc or Edu check, the dock administrator will give the player characters access to monitor the incoming and outgoing freight canisters.

With a successful Average (+0) Computers, Edu or Int check, the player characters can set their portacomp to monitor canister movement and notify them if another canister goes missing. Alternately, the player characters can make a Simple (+6) Recon, Int or Een, 2D days, skill test to monitor them manually.

If the player characters want to question Ermir Leka, go to Questioning the Docker on pg. 49.

If the player characters monitor the movement of canisters on the Red Section apron for at least a week, go to Caught in the Act on pg. 51.

Questioning the Docker

If the player characters bring Ermir Leka in for questioning, he will have a union lawyer accompany him. Player characters will need to succeed on an Average (+0) Advocate, Edu or Soc check to negotiate past the lawyer.

If the player characters question Leka about how he was identified in the system as being the docker who checked in the ore canister containing the victims' remains, he will turn pale. A successful Average (+0) Persuade, Soc check will get Leka pleading his innocence in the matter and that he was in no way a part of killing people or hiding bodies. He will tell the player characters that the Red Section docks radio-frequency ID security system is extremely overdue for an upgrade. A year ago the dockers discovered they could clone a co-worker's badge with some off-the-shelf electronics. This let them 'clock in' their friends, making it appear someone was at work and eligible for pay when, in reality, that someone was truant and hanging out at the Bawdy Lass. When Baczkowski discovered what was going on he put a stop to it, saying it was a disgrace to the union.

The Manufacturer

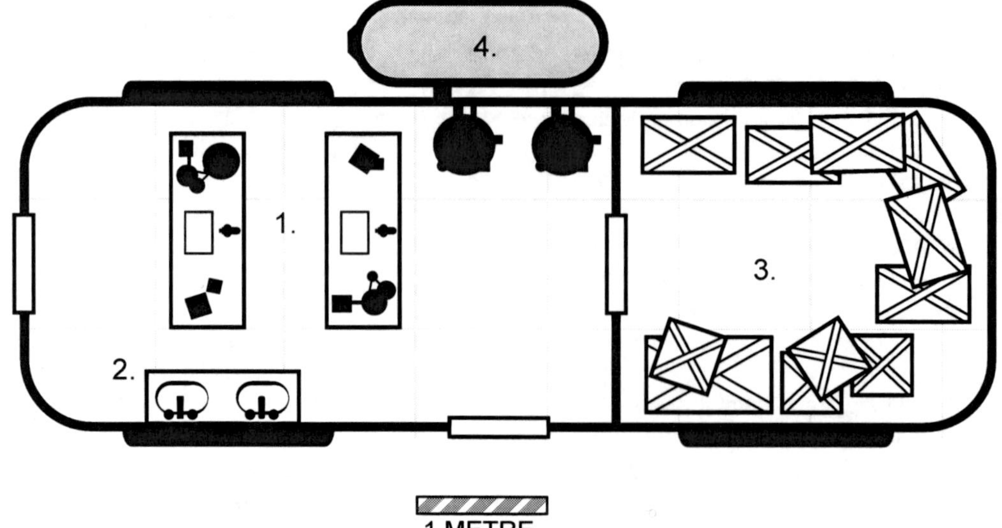

If the player characters successfully interrogate Samuel Wan or shadow his movement through the spaceport, they will discover a drug lab has been set up in an untravelled area of Orange Section. From a construction module, Wan and other dealers on the station purchase product from an individual by the name of Nash. Wan knows that Nash employs a pair of chemists who produce Scribble in the module itself. He also knows that Nash usually has four or five guards with him at all times. He does not believe the guards carry firearms but knows they are plenty deadly with knives and hooks.

A successful Simple (+6) Admin, Int or Edu check will reveal that the construction module is owned by Tone-Kant Construction, an American subsidiary owned by the German conglomerate Baustoffe. Tone-Kant is one of several subcontractors at Boise that are engaged in light pre-development work, including surveying the mineralogical composition of the asteroid. If the player characters want to legally search the module, they will need to have a warrant from AUSA Park.

Cole Nash, the brains behind the Scribble manufacturing operation on Boise, is a middle-tier T-K site manager. Tapping company resources he has established his own illegal side business. He has set up a pair of chemists in a Tone-Kant construction module on Boise and hired several contract labourers as part-time enforcers. The operation, away from prying eyes and camouflaged as legitimate spaceport activity, has been a quiet success. Items go missing from Tone-Kant's on-site chemical stores on a regular basis so keeping drug manufacturing supplies in stock has been easy for Nash's crew.

The entrance to the module is guarded around the clock by two construction workers stationed just outside. Two more are located inside. Use the Spaceport Worker sample NPC, pg. 278 of *2300AD*, but replace Gun Combat (slug rifle) 2 with Melee (armed) 2. Each guard carries a large utility knife that functions as a dagger. The guards know that drug manufacturing is a mandatory mind wipe so they will fight the player characters as if they have nothing to lose. Nash and the chemists are Average Non-combatants and will attempt to flee the scene if they can.

The construction module consists of two rooms: one equipped with chemical burners and other pieces of lab paraphernalia and the other used for storage. If the player characters examine the module after securing it, a successful Average (+0) Investigate, Int, 1 day, check will allow them to piece together what is going on. Alternately, the player characters can attempt an opposed Persuade, Soc or Str vs. Nash's Deception, Soc check.

While busting the drug lab will earn the player characters the gratitude of the Ellis State Police, the lab itself is a dead end as Nash has no direct connection to the dockers. However, if the player characters question Nash, on a successful Easy (+2) Persuade, Soc check, Nash will be willing to give up information in exchange for leniency. According to the rumour mill, an exo-loader named 'Kady' or 'Michelle' was responsible for the murder of the Mahal & Loke employees.

Caught in the Act

After a week of monitoring, the player characters will notice that six canisters were delivered to the incorrect dock aprons. Of those, all but one were shifted back by Emir Leka. If the player characters have questioned Leka (see Questioning the Docker on pg. 49), Michael Baczkowski will take on this role. Either Leka/Baczkowski is amazingly good at finding mistakes or he is involved with suspicious activities.

If the player characters decide to shadow Leka/Baczkowski, a successful Average (+0) Stealth, Dex or Int, 4 hours, check will allow the player characters to keep tabs on him without drawing attention. If the player characters watch Leka/Baczkowski on the docks while simultaneously monitor the inventory system they will observe the following:

1. While in the high-security area of the dock apron, Leka/Baczkowski will scan a canister.
2. The scanned canister will be removed from the dock's inventory system.
3. Utilising a Hump-It exo-suit, Leka will pick up the scanned canister and carry it to the low-security apron.
4. Thirty minutes later, another Hump-It, this one piloted by a square-jawed blonde man, will enter the low-security apron, pick up the canister and carry it off to the aprons.

If the player characters follow the canister, a successful Average (+0) Stealth, Dex or Int check will allow them quietly shadow the Hump-It driver to warehouse R-12 in Red Section.

If the player characters ask the Hump-It driver for identification he will be identified as Mischa Cadiz, a licensed exo-suit driver and contract day labourer. Cadiz's permanent address is in Liberty on Ellis but he rents an apartment in Red Section. If the player characters wish to avoid contact, a camera-captured snapshot and a successful Simple (+6) Admin, Int or Edu check will reveal the same information.

If the player characters follow up on Cadiz, go to Mischa Cadiz.

If the player characters investigate the warehouse, go to Big Pig Warehousing on pg. 52.

Mischa Cadiz

If the player characters want to bring Mischa Cadiz in for questioning, they will need to tie him directly to a criminal conspiracy. If the player characters arrested and questioned Nash, they will have the name of a suspected murder named 'Kady' or 'Michelle.' The name Mischa Cadiz is too close to be a coincidence. If the player characters run the name by Nash, he will tell them that it sounds about right.

If the player characters review surveillance footage of the Mahal & Loke employees going through Boise Customs visa processing the day of their murder, a successful Routine (+2) Int check will reveal that Cadiz was standing nearby.

The player characters can keep watch on Cadiz and track his movements. A successful Routine (+2) Recon, End or Int, 2D+2 days check will reveal the following: Each time Ermir Leka or Michael Baczkowski remove a canister from the dock inventory system, Cadiz picks it up in the low-security apron and carries the erased canister to Big Pig Warehousing. If the player characters are able to follow the movement of the canister into the warehouse (see Big Pig Warehousing on pg. 52).

If the player characters successfully file for a search warrant of Mischa Cadiz's residence, they will discover several pieces of electronic equipment and blank RFID badges. A successful Simple (+6) Physical Science (electronics) check, will reveal that this gear has been used to create spoofed RFID badges and the last badge spoofed was Ermir Leka's.

If the player characters arrest Mischa Cadiz for murder, he will reveal, in exchange for a reduced sentence, that he is part of a bigger group. AUSA Xander Park will agree to consider the exchange depending on what Cadiz reveals. Cadiz explains that he is employed by a man named Zachariah Modine. While Cadiz is not political, he knows that his boss is the leader of a New America terror cell. Modine has been setting up a New America base of operations in Beech Grove Canyons, outside of Liberty. Modine dispatched Cadiz to the Sol system to hire engineers who would help get the base up and running. Modine hired the engineers, brought them to Ellis and handed them over to Modine. Nine months later, Modine told Cadiz to dispose of the engineers. He lured them to a Big Pig Warehouse and, with some muscle-for-hire, they were killed. Using a spoofed RFID badge, they carried the bodies through service corridors and stuffed them in ore canisters. The idea was to get the bodies into the ore bins where they would be crushed and irretrievable.

Cadiz spends most of his time at Boise Spaceport and handles arriving contraband deliveries. Union dockers named Leka and Baczkowski shift certain containers from the Customs era to the low security dock apron. From there Cadiz picks them up and takes them to Big Pig Warehousing where they are shipped to Ellis. Cadiz suspects the contraband is weaponry and supplies and doubts that the dockers know what is in them. Or that they would even want to know.

Big Pig Warehouse

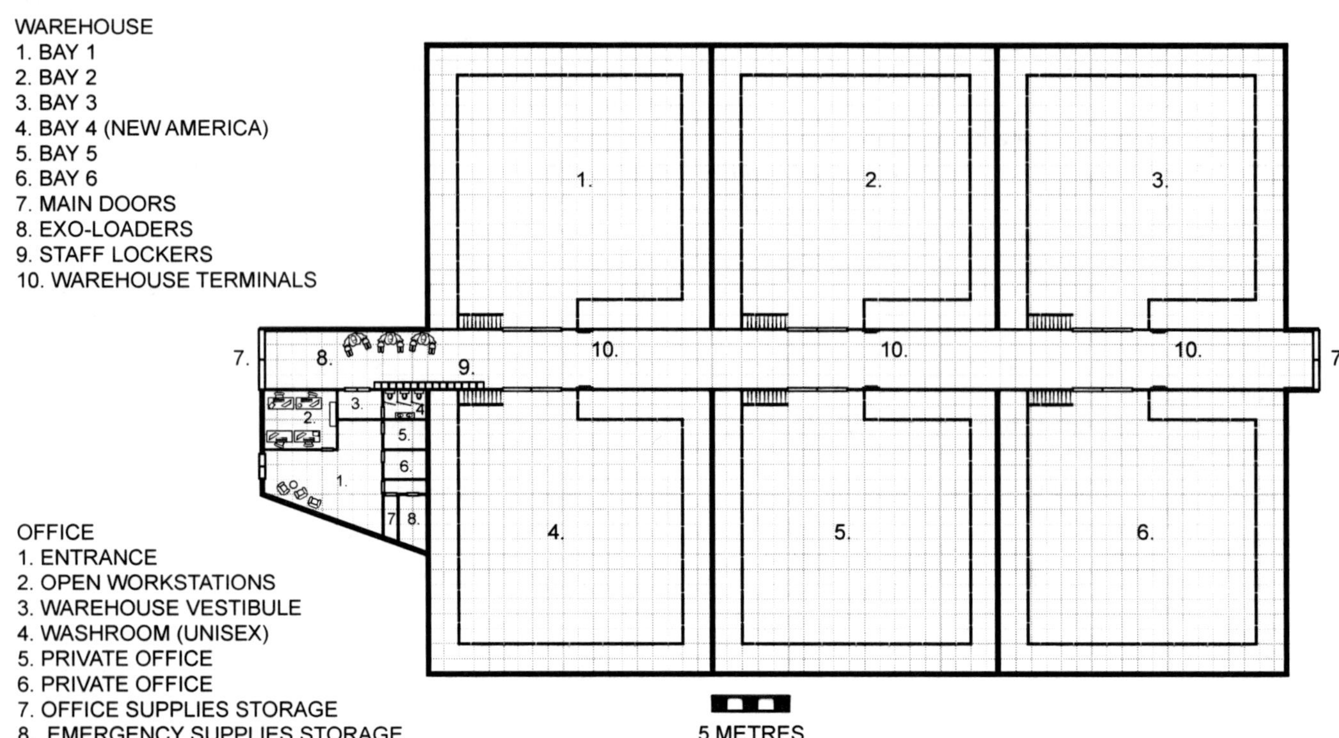

Big Pig Warehousing is a network of six massive storage spaces. The company prides itself on providing variable temperature control for cargoes heading for and leaving Ellis. A successful Easy (+4) Admin, Int or Edu check will reveal that the owner and manager of Big Pig Warehousing is Dean Pileggi.

If the player characters have been investigating dockside canister movement (see Following the Canisters on pg. 48), they should make a Simple (+6) Computers, Int or Soc check. On success, the player characters learn from corroborating data that each time an item disappears from the Red Section dock inventory, Big Pig Warehousing is contacted via Link. The spaceport's communication system routers do not record conversations, only who called who, but the connection is important in that it links the two.

Contraband shipments destined for Zachariah Modine's new command post pass through the warehouse to shuttles that transport the goods to Ellis. From the Liberty Spaceport, trucks owned by Modine pick up the canisters and they are driven out to Beech Grove Canyons. It may be tempting for player characters to storm the warehouse with a warrant and flip open every container but AUSA Xander Park and SSA Karli Kapinos will tell them the smarter move would be to discover the cargo canisters' final destinations. If the player characters would like to infiltrate the warehouse, a successful application for a search warrant and/or electronic surveillance warrant will keep their actions legal.

Big Pig Warehousing consists of six large bays connected by a central corridor for moving canisters in and out. The main warehouse door is large enough to accommodate exo-loaders and other manned cargo carriers. A small service door leads to the warehouse office. With the exception of Bay 4, all of these doors are equipped with Easy (+4) electronic lock systems. There are 2D+3 warehouse workers working at any given time. Use the Spaceport Worker sample NPC from pg. 279 of *2300AD*.

Pileggi has set aside Bay 4 of the warehouse for New America contraband shipments. It utilises a different electronic lock system from the rest of the warehouse (Routine +2) and is physically guarded by an enforcer disguised as a warehouse worker. Use the Petty Thug sample NPC from pg. 84 of the *Traveller Core Rulebook* and arm him with a dagger. A successful opposed Social Science (psychology), Int or Soc vs. Deception, Soc check will allow the player characters to see past the disguise.

Once inside Bay 4, if the player characters examine the bay's canister manifests they will notice that the final delivery locations do not correspond to any actual coordinates in the colony. If they open a canister, they will discover black market military assault rifles from the Chinese Arm. Successfully affixing RFID tags to the canisters requires a Simple (+6) Physical Sciences (electronics), Int or Dex check.

If the player characters have been tipped to Pileggi's involvement by other suspects, the player characters may choose to bring him in for questioning. Pileggi is in his early 40s and sports a shaved head and olive complexion. He will deny any accusation until the player characters actually discover contraband in his warehouse. If the player characters bring this evidence to light, Pileggi will admit to being a member of New America. On a successful Very Difficult (-4) Persuade, Soc check, Pileggi will tell the player characters that Zachariah Modine, the Liberty area New America commander, has been building a command post in Beech Grove Canyons stocked with enough food, water and weapons to wage a war. When the time for revolution comes, Modine plans to order an assault on the Ellis state capitol.

When the player characters are ready to have the canisters traced, go to The Canyons.

The Canyons

Due to the size of their batteries, even the best RFID tags still have a limited broadcast range of 2,000 meters. The NSO does not have the hardware or resources to monitor in-system ship traffic. However, if they coordinate with the Interstellar Commerce Monitoring Network (ICMN) they can use ICMN's radio frequency tracking system to keep tabs on the shuttle.

When the player characters are ready to monitor the RFID-tagged contraband canisters, they should contact ICMN. Sharing their RFID frequency and a successful Routine (+2) Leadership, Soc check will convince ICMN technicians at Boise and on Ellis to cooperate. Until the canisters leave the station via shuttle, the player characters can keep tabs on them via their portacomp.

After 1D+2 days, the canisters in Bay 4 of Big Pig Warehousing will be moved to Red Section docks and loaded aboard an outbound cargo shuttle. If the player characters have successfully brought in ICMN's assistance, they can return to Ellis's surface aboard a passenger shuttle. Daring player characters may attempt to smuggle themselves aboard the shuttle to keep watch on the canisters. The cargo bay is pressurised but the trip down to the surface will be very rough. The player characters will need to jury-rig some sort of restraint system with a successful Difficult (-2) Physical Science (physics) or Life Science (biology), Int or Edu, 1 day, check to keep themselves from injury.

After descending through Ellis's atmosphere, the cargo shuttle will land at Liberty Spaceport. Following decontamination procedures, cargo will be off-loaded and moved to warehousing where it will wait for pickup. Within 1D+2 hours, a pair of Iltis 3.5 wheeled 6×6 cargo trucks (pg. 175, *2300AD*) arrive and the canisters are loaded into the back of the trucks. From there, begins an hours long drive south to Beech Grove Canyons.

If they call ahead, SSA Karli Kapinos will have a Houston Motors Rangestar waiting for them at the spaceport. In the player characters' favour, a light dust storm has begun to blow in the region. The particulate matter will help hide the player characters' vehicle from the truck drivers. However, the player characters will need to make a successful Average (+0) Sensors, Int or Edu check to keep tabs on the trucks. The player characters vehicle will also need to remain within 2 kilometres of the cargo trucks, requiring a successful Routine (+2) Drive (wheeled), Dex check.

When the cargo trucks arrive at Beech Grove Canyons, they will turn off onto a gravel ramp leading down into the canyon floor. Moments later the RFID signals will cease transmitting, as if blocked somehow. A successful Average (+0) Recon, Int or Edu check will allow the player characters to accurately mark the coordinates where the vehicles disappeared. For the time being, the characters can do nothing further than return to the NSO field office in Liberty. As they approach the city, they will receive a National Weather Service warning of an approaching dust storm with wind speeds that will exceed 100km/h. Go to Storming the Bunker.

Storming the Bunker

When the player characters return to the NSO field office, SSA Karli Kapinos will be leading a satellite and aerial drone analysis of the area the player characters marked in Beech Grove Canyons. US government satellites have begun peppering the surface of the canyon with thermal imaging and ground penetrating radar. It is soon discovered that some sort of underground New America bunker facility has been constructed inside the canyon wall. Disguised solar cell panels, vents and radiators have been identified at the surface. A gravel ramp leads down to the bottom of the canyon where individuals armed with assault rifles guard the entrance. Radar has identified four levels, with some sort of garage or motor pool and water pump station on the canyon floor level. The middle two levels appear to be barracks and the top level contains power systems and is linked directly to the panelling on the 'roof.'

After time to recoup, the player characters are called into a briefing at the field office which is led by ASAC John Nieten, the regional NSO SWAT commander. The player characters are being pulled in to assist on a strike of the New America base that will coincide with the large dust storm now blowing through the area. The player characters skills will determine how they participate. Any character with the Drive (walker) skill will be offered the use of a Bulldog battlesuit (see pg. 31, *Hard Suits, Combat Walkers and Battlesuits*).

The assault will be two pronged, with a battlesuit team storming the main entrance and a stealth team punching through the surface ventilation system and working its way down. An air assault is out of the question so the NSO SWAT force will be carried from Liberty to the edge of Beech Grove Canyons in a pair of Mulecorp Explorer ATVs. At one kilometre's distance from the canyon edge, the two teams will deploy using the dust storm for cover. The battlesuit team will make its way to the canyon floor while the stealth team moves into position above the power generation level. At the signal, both will commence their attack. Nieten advises all the Special Agents that they have no idea what possible chemical, biological or radiological devices New America may have on hand at this time so the assault team is authorised to shoot first and ask questions later.

The player characters and NPCs will be issued Stracher MP-67 submachine guns with 8 additional magazines, a set of full-body inertial armour, helmets with internal displays and limited atmospheric filters, and up to six smoke, gas, flash-bang and/or stun grenades. Any player characters who wish to take on a sniper role will be issued a Rockwell 12-81 Magnum rifle with 6 additional magazines. Use the Mercenary sample NPC from pg. 280, *2300AD* for the 8 NSO SWAT Special Agents.

The Base

The New America bunker consists of four levels of steel-reinforced concrete and stone built into the western escarpment of Beech Grove Canyons. The bunker was designed to take advantage of the aquifer located far below and, as it is hidden in a canyon, designed to be as difficult to find and detect as possible. As Ellis lacks mountainous terrain, terrorists will hide in low places rather than from elevated positions. Thankfully for the player characters, the New America bunker is designed more as a hiding place than a true fort. A ground-penetrating missile strike would easily destroy it but that type of hardware is limited to the American military. Counter-terror operations on American soil is the jurisdiction of the NSO.

At the top of the canyon, a wide and winding gravel ramp system, averaging at a 30° degree incline, leads to the canyon floor. Bulldozers and graders have levelled the floor of the

canyon allowing for wheeled and hover vehicles to easily traverse it. Vehicles traversing down the gravel ramp will be under constant surveillance. As Beech Grove Canyons were formed from slow wind erosion, they are not particularly deep. From the lip of the canyon edge to the floor, the height averages 15 metres. It is possible for skilfully piloted battlesuits to safely and quickly traverse the steep terrain using winches on a successful Average (+0) Drive (walker) check.

The entrance to the bunker is situated behind a 8.8 metre × 6.9 metre high blast door. However, the blast door's mechanical system has not been installed yet so it is left open. Beyond the blast door is the bunker's ground floor garage area, primary armoury and water pump station. There are typically 2D+1 armed New America soldiers patrolling inside and just beyond the garage perimeter. Use the Terrorist sample NPC from pg. 279 of *2300AD* and add the Dry World DNAM. Equip each with a Wu-Beijing Type-49 Assault Rifle. With every fourth terrorist, equip him with a Yen Shan State Armoury Type-81 Storm Gun. All terrorists are also equipped with desert survival clothing including goggles and water packs.

Parked in the garage are a pair of Iltis 3.5 cargo trucks, three American Motors Sierra off-road technical trucks, two of which sport mounted Wu-Beijing Type 381 Machineguns in their beds, and a Ma'iingan off-road motorcycle (see *Tools for Frontier Living* for more information on these vehicles). Also parked in a garage are the remains of a Lynx armoured vehicle that has had its armour stripped down to the frame and its engine block removed. The engine hangs on a chain from the ceiling. Various machine parts, blow torches, welding gear and mechanic's tools litter the garage floor.

Behind the garage is a personnel elevator and staircase that runs through all four levels of the bunker. Next to the elevator is the bunker's primary armoury. The armoury is half stocked with black market firearms, crates of grenades and commercial mining explosives and three LAW-66 rocket launchers. After the second round of the assault, 3 terrorists will run for the rocket launchers and attempt to fire them at the NSO Bulldogs.

Next to the armoury is the water pump station. Six Trilon TRj20 water pump units pull moisture from the underground aquifer and fill several large storage tanks. Two additional pumps sit unopened in crates nearby.

The second level of the bunker is the staging level. Here, New America soldiers gather for briefings, recreation and to do personal equipment checks and maintenance. Next to the staging area is the bunker's communications suite, a holotank unit still sitting unassembled in its shipping container and three offices, one of which is set aside for Zachariah Modine. The majority of the New America cell's operations are kept in the heads of its leaders rather than committed to paper or electronic media but Modine has an affectation for maps and lists. If the player characters search his office they will find several maps of the immediate area which outline various proposed terrorist operations in Liberty including bombing the Federal Complex and the capitol building. They also find lists of assassination targets, including the Ellis State Police commandant, the governor and key members of the state legislature.

There are 2D+6 terrorists on the second floor. If they are taken by surprise, half of them (round up) be carrying only Traylor Model 57 pistols. One round following an attack, they will make for assault rifles scattered about the floor. By round four, all will be armed.

The third level of the bunker consists of living quarters (bunks for common soldiers and private rooms for 'non-coms') and a large mess and kitchen. The kitchen freezer is well stocked with food stuffs. This level also has a smaller armoury which contains personal firearms, boxes of ammunition and various pieces of survival gear. There are 1D+8 terrorists on this level.

The fourth level is a large open space containing power plants, generators and HVAC systems. Power cables drop from the ceiling and are connected to solar cells in the terrain above. The power plants and air-intake vents are connected above as well and are hidden underneath camouflage tarps. In the ceiling of this level is a drop-ladder leading to an escape hatch to the surface. A successful Difficult (-2) Investigation, Int, 1D minute(s) skill test will reveal the presence of the hatch. A successful Average (+0) Mechanic, Int or Edu check will allow a player character to by-pass the mechanical lock.

What About Baczkowski?

After the contraband smuggling operations at Boise Spaceport are revealed to the public, Michael Baczkowski will be forced to step down from his position of union secretary-treasurer in disgrace. To avoid prison, he will cut a deal with law enforcement to share everything he knows about how smugglers have been using the spaceport to sneak contraband through. While this will be considered a victory, criminal outfits will simply find alternate channels to get their cargoes through.

Ivan Dekker will easily win the union leadership election but the union will face tough decisions. Without Baczkowski's slush funds the union is going to face a loss of political support and calls for more automation.